10 Questions:
A Deep Look at Yourself Through Poetry

Kerry Wald

Copyright ©2025
All rights reserved. Written permission must be secured from the author to reproduce any part of the book.

Printed in the United States of America

ISBN: 979-8-3484-9691-3

10 9 8 7 6 5 4 3 2 1

EMPIRE PUBLISHING
www.empirebookpublishing.com

Dedication

To those who dare to look within,
who brave the shadows and embrace the light,

this book is for you.

To the seekers of the truth,
the warriors of self-reflection,
and the dreamers who believe in the power of words.

May these pages be a companion on your journey,
a mirror to your soul,
and a spark to the fire that burns within you.

With gratitude for your courage,
and in honor of your continued growth,
this book is dedicated to you.

Welcome to Explore10Questions.com

Discover 10 Questions: A Deep Look at Yourself Through Poetry, a book designed to guide you through self-reflection and personal growth. Here, you can learn more about the book, read about its unique approach, and purchase your copy.

10QuestionsJournal.com: Your Private Reflection Space

To help you on your personal journey, we created 10QuestionsJournal.com—a secure, private platform where you can log in, answer each question from the book, and revisit your thoughts over time.

How It Works:

- Your Private Journal: When you purchase 10 Questions, you gain access to 10QuestionsJournal.com, where you'll create a personal account with a password. This space is completely private—only you can access your entries.

- Return & Reflect: After answering the questions, you can return to your journal any time to review, add to, or modify your reflections. Whether it's a few weeks or months later, you'll be able to track your growth and revisit the thoughts that shaped you.

- Your Thoughts, anywhere: No matter where you are, your reflections are with you. Whether you're on the go or at home, you can log in to reflect, add new insights, or simply decompress by writing when life feels heavy. It's a way to clear your mind and put words to emotions that may be difficult to process.

Why Explore10Questions.com?

Life can be chaotic, and sometimes our thoughts get lost in the noise. This site is a place where you can come back to your center. From learning more about the book to accessing your personal journal, Explore10Questions.com is your home base for reflection and growth.

Personal Introduction to "10 Questions: A Deep Look at Yourself Through Poetry"

Born in the vibrant heart of Las Vegas into a life of privilege, my early years were shaped by extraordinary experiences and opportunities. As the son of a distinguished army general and a prominent casino president, I was immersed in an environment filled with love, faith, and the diverse tapestry of human connections that only a city like Las Vegas can offer. Surrounded by supportive family members and friends, I enjoyed a childhood marked by world travels and cultural riches, learning invaluable lessons from each adventure and every soul I encountered.

Yet, life has a way of testing our foundations. The stability and comforts of my youth were profoundly shaken by my parents' divorce, stripping away the material ease and forcing me to confront a new reality—one where the abundance I took for granted was replaced by the need to fend for myself. Through these trials, I learned not just the value of money, but the deeper worth of resilience and independence.

Transitioning from the silver spoons of youth to the wooden spoons of adversity, I found solace and expression in the world of bartending. With a degree in psychology in hand, I spent 27 years listening to the life stories told across the polished bar tops—stories of joy, despair, and everything in between. Each conversation was a window into another life, providing me with a broader understanding of the universal struggles and triumphs we all share.

It was from this rich reservoir of shared human experience that I found my true calling in writing. What began as a personal coping mechanism—scribbling words to soothe my own turmoil—soon morphed into a powerful tool for healing. My writings, often spontaneous and raw, seemed to weave the problems presented at the bar into poetic solutions that resonated with both the writer and the reader. The act of writing became a form of release and discovery, a way to navigate through the stormy seas of life's challenges.

This book, "10 Questions: A Deep Look at Yourself Through Poetry," is a culmination of these experiences. Crafted under the unique structure of the rule of three—each section invites you to read a thought-provoking quote, reflect on a corresponding artwork, and delve into a poem that mirrors the complexities of human emotions. Following each poem are ten reflective questions designed to challenge and inspire you. This interactive format is not just about reading; it's about engaging actively with your thoughts and feelings, encouraging a dialogue within yourself that is both transformative and enlightening.

My hope is that this book reaches anyone who seeks understanding and strength in their journey. Whether you are a young adult just starting to shape your own story, or someone well-versed in the narratives of life, here you will find a space to reflect, learn, and grow. "10 Questions" is more than a book; it's a companion on the road to self-discovery, a guide that illuminates the paths of resilience and self-belief.

Through the pages of this book, I invite you to explore not only the poetry and its accompanying imagery but also to discover the power of self-reflection. This journey is about unlocking the doors to your own depths, confronting your fears, and embracing your potential to lead a life marked by purpose and introspection.

Welcome to a profound exploration of self, where each question leads you closer to the answers that lie within, ready to be uncovered and understood.

"10 Questions: A Deep Look at Yourself Through Poetry" is more than just a book; it is a deeply personal exploration into the essence of who you are. Within its pages, you are invited to embark on a journey of self-reflection, where the layers of your inner world are gently peeled back to reveal the truths that lie within. This book serves as a mirror, reflecting the complexities of your thoughts, emotions, and experiences, challenging you to confront and understand the different facets of your identity.

The structure of this exploration is grounded in the rule of three—a picture, a quote, and a poem. Each chapter carefully weaves these elements together, creating a rich tapestry that guides you through the process of introspection. The picture sets the scene, offering a visual cue that evokes certain emotions and memories. The quote provides wisdom or perspective, serving as a lens through which you can view your own experiences. The poem, the heart of each chapter, delves deep into the core of the theme, offering a lyrical exploration of the question at hand. This triad creates a holistic approach to self-exploration, engaging both your intellect and your emotions.

This book goes beyond surface-level reflection. It delves into the often challenging aspects of personal growth, addressing themes like insecurity, unhealthy thinking patterns, and the loss of motivation. These are the shadows that many of us carry, often unnoticed or unaddressed, yet they profoundly impact our lives. Through poetry, this book offers a compassionate yet unflinching look at these issues, encouraging you to face them head-on.

As you navigate these ten questions, you are encouraged to not only absorb the insights presented but to also contribute your own. This is a deeply interactive process—one that asks you to actively engage with the material and draw your own conclusions. Your personal insights, reflections, and even your struggles become part of the narrative, making this book as unique as your own journey. It is a space where you can explore your thoughts, confront your insecurities, challenge unhealthy thinking, and rediscover the motivation that may have waned. In essence, "10 Questions: A Deep Look at Yourself Through Poetry" is a conversation with yourself, a tool for self-discovery, and a catalyst for personal growth. It is designed to help you uncover the layers of your being, to understand who you are, and to find the strength and clarity to move forward on your path. As you turn each page, may you find not only answers but also new questions that inspire deeper reflection and continued growth, guiding you toward a more authentic and fulfilled life.

Table of Contents

Chapter 1: Time 3
    Timeless 6
    10 Questions to Reflect On, ... 8

Chapter 2: Faith 10
    Faith or Failure 13
    10 Questions to Reflect On, ... 16

Chapter 3: Follower or Leader 18
    The End Is The Beginning 21
    10 Questions to Reflect On, ... 23

Chapter 4: Drained 25
    Drained 28
    10 Questions to Reflect On, ... 31

Chapter 5: Mirror 33
    Mirror 36
    10 Questions to Reflect On, ... 39

Chapter 6: As I Rise 43
    As I Rise 46
    10 Questions to Reflect On, ... 48

Chapter 7: Infidelity 50
    Confessions of a Madman 53

10 Questions to Reflect On, ... 57

Chapter 8: Resilience 59
Pinnacle 62
10 Questions to Reflect On, ... 65

Chapter 9: Change 67
The Lonely Road of Change 70
10 Questions to Reflect On, ... 74

Chapter 10: Life Is The Secret 79
The Secret 82
10 Questions to Reflect On, ... 85

Chapter 11: Prison Of Yesterday 87
Signs 90
10 Questions to Reflect On, ... 92

Chapter 12: Friend or Fair Weather 94
Yes 97
10 Questions to Reflect On, ... 101

Chapter 13: The Challenge Of Life 103
A Tale Written in the Stars 106
10 Questions to Reflect On, ... 108

Chapter 14: Loss 110
The Pain Remains 113

10 Questions to Reflect On, ...117

Chapter 15: Unmasked 121
    The Show 124
    10 Questions to Reflect On, ...126

Chapter 16: Temptation vs. Inner Strength...128
    Torment..131
    10 Questions to Reflect On, ...133

Chapter 17: Breaking The Cycle..135
    The Mill 139
    10 Questions to Reflect On, ...141

Chapter 18: Embracing The Journey 143
    The Human Adventure 147
    10 Questions to Reflect On, ...151

Chapter 19: Strength In Hope 153
    Hope Has Brought You Out 157
    10 Questions to Reflect On, ...160

Chapter 20: United In Purpose, Divided by Perception 162
    Why..166
    10 Questions to Reflect On, ...170

Chapter 21: Consumptions Downfall 172
    A Realm of Fire 176

10 Questions to Reflect On, ... 179

Chapter 22: Forgotten Souls 181

    Left Behind and Broken 184

    10 Questions to Reflect On, ... 187

Chapter 23: 189

    Explanation of Transitional Images: Open Doorways 189

About the Author 197

Chapter 1: Time

Time is the one constant that governs all of life's experiences. From the moment we are born, it begins its unyielding march forward, affecting every aspect of who we are and what we do. We are always in a hurry—rushing to meet deadlines, achieve goals, and reach the next milestone. Yet, no matter how fast we move, time often feels elusive, as if there is never enough of it to fully accomplish all we desire. We chase after the future, sacrificing the present, and before we realize it, childhood slips into memory, and we find ourselves on the other side of life's hill, wondering how the years passed so quickly.

As we grow older, time becomes a bittersweet companion. In our youth, it seems abundant, stretching out like an infinite horizon. We are eager to grow up, to experience everything, often not realizing how swiftly it passes until it's too late. As we age, we begin to feel the weight of time more acutely. We lose people we love, feel the creeping limitations of our bodies, and face the reality that time is finite. It shapes how we eat, sleep, and live, reminding us that our moments are precious and few. In the end, time governs not just our schedules, but our very existence, leaving us to navigate its currents while trying to make the most of the fleeting minutes we are given.

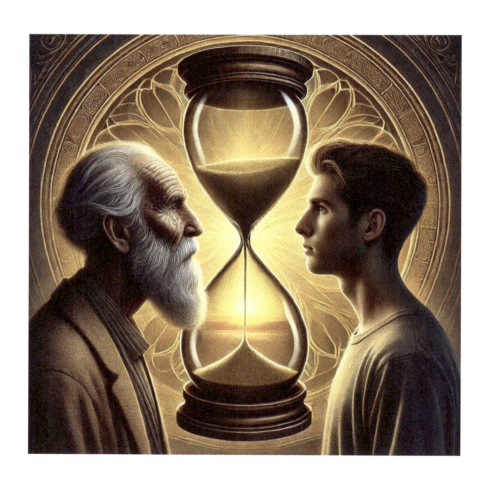

Timeless

Time, most precious gift we have, because it is the one thing we cannot create or recover once it's lost. Every moment is an opportunity to grow, to love, to make a difference. Like a collection of these moments, woven together by the choices we make, and the paths we choose to follow. Time teaches us that nothing is permanent, that change is inevitable, and that we must cherish the fleeting beauty of each day. The true measure of life is not in the number of years we live, but in the richness of the experiences we embrace and the legacy we leave behind.

—Unknown

Timeless

Time is listening.
The moments careen about my wayward mind,
Crowned and cornered,
Shaking with rage.
A distinction to believe in—
How far away?
A journey of endlessness.

The hunger of an unavailing current,
Multiple directions,
No set course,
Only a feeling in a reminiscent dream.

Look inside the darkness,
Past the murk and mystery.
What is missing?
Clarity in your direction.
Your feelings are the compass.
Will fuels your fortitude—
A prelude to an epic undertaking.

One moment, separated from the rest,
Put together, a puzzle with misplaced pieces.
Clouded and vague,
Secluded from triumph.
Realizing your foolishness,
You acquire guidance.

If we disentangle and decipher,
Seconds are lost to minutes.
Minutes are slaves to hours.
Hours are disciples of days.
Days are students of months.
Months instruct and guide years.
Years clarify and remind through introspection.

We shape and mold our chronology.
Our lives are a continuance of multiple instances.
We are the witnesses and actors,
Briefly seeing from all sides,
Portraying and feeling everything.
Following every feeling, time is departing.

The lessons we learn are everything we have never known or will ever know.
Time affords glimpses of our possibilities.
Timelessness reflects in your eyes as it expires.
You can't purchase more,
Barter for extensions.
Only your spirit lives on within your reflection.

Don't stress on time, watching it slip away.
Embrace every moment you have.
Experience everything you can.
Make each engagement not lived in time,
But lived timelessly.

Timeless

10 Questions to Reflect On,

1. How do you prioritize your time daily to ensure you're focusing on what truly matters to you?
   - What distractions or habits do you need to let go of to create more space for your true priorities?
2. Can you recall a moment when you realized the irreversible nature of time, and how did it change your approach to life?
   - How has this realization impacted the way you make decisions or handle opportunities that come your way?
3. In what ways have you grown from the opportunities that each moment has presented to you?
   - How do you ensure you're staying open to new opportunities, even when they may not seem significant at first?
4. How do you find balance between making lasting memories and the everyday responsibilities?
   - What strategies or boundaries help you carve out time for meaningful experiences amid daily obligations?
5. What are some examples of how you've used your time to make a difference in someone else's life?
   - How can you continue to make an impact, no matter how small, in the lives of others?
6. How do you measure the 'richness' of your experiences? Is it through joy, learning, or something else?

- What can you do to enhance the depth and meaning of your experiences moving forward?

7. Looking back, which choices do you believe have significantly shaped your life's path?
    - How do you think your life would be different if you'd made alternative choices, and what have you learned from this reflection?

8. How do you prepare yourself for inevitable changes in life?
    - What practices help you stay adaptable and resilient in the face of uncertainty and change?

9. What legacy do you hope to leave behind, and how are your daily actions aligned with this goal?
    - What adjustments can you make today to ensure that your actions align more closely with the legacy you want to build?

10. Reflecting on the 'fleeting beauty of each day,' what small moments recently have you cherished the most?
    - How can you cultivate more awareness and appreciation for the simple, beautiful moments in each day?

Chapter 2: Faith

Faith in ourselves is one of the most powerful forces we can possess, yet it is often the hardest to nurture. Believing in who we are and what we are capable of requires courage, especially in a world that constantly tests our resolve. Doubts creep in, failures seem to confirm our fears, and obstacles arise that make us question whether we are strong enough to overcome them. But it is precisely in these moments of uncertainty that we discover what it means to truly believe in ourselves. When everything around us seems to falter, faith becomes a lifeline—a quiet but unshakable inner voice that urges us to keep moving forward, to rise despite our fears, and to continue striving for what we know deep inside we are meant to achieve.

Finding this inner strength takes time and resilience. Often, it is only when we are pushed to the brink, when we feel like giving up, that we truly learn what we are capable of. The fight for faith in ourselves is not easy; many things get in our way—failures, criticism, self-doubt—but these challenges also teach us to push harder. With each setback, we uncover more of our willpower, learn to trust our instincts, and find the courage to continue. Faith is not a passive belief; it is an active, ongoing battle to claim our worth and potential, especially when the world or even our own thoughts try to convince us otherwise. It is in this fight that we grow stronger, and through it, we come to believe in ourselves more fully than we ever imagined.

Faith Or Failure

"Faith in yourself is the beacon that guides you through the darkest storms of failure. Even when the world seems to crumble around you, that inner belief gives you the strength to rise, to fight, and to become more than you ever imagined. It is in those moments of doubt and defeat that your true power emerges—shaping not just your destiny, but the lives of others, creating a legacy of resilience and impact."

— Unknown

Faith or Failure

Faith in the faithless—a failing.
An opportunity for inconsistent change.
It used to be a malleable option,
Molded and comforted,
Lost to indecision and distorted equilibrium.

Time and time again, we are convinced.
Always the same,
Believing the outcome will be different.
Withdrawn in private silence,
Ashamed, outnumbered by the rabble,
Numb to the exposure.

Finding your assurance—
Is it real?
Hit the wall with conviction.
The same is adrift and purposeless,
Offering nothing of choice,
Forced into sorrow
When faith is vacant.

What is the arrangement?
How awkward the occasion—
A summons in an ordinary world
By an extraordinary calling.

How will you escape your falseness?
A wondrous failure of your own demise,

An empty shill with finite chances,
Matching monsters and demons,
Despair and sorrow,
Easily repaired.

It begins in silence—
Pure clarity,
Monumental vision.
It won't be easy.
Release the chains.
Nothing is undone.

It might seem all is lost—
Sorrow faultlessly encompassing,
A deluge that never ends,
Only heartache and pain.

No words, only empty and faithless.
The end is a minefield.
Time is remorseless,
Screaming for help,
Day by day starving at your reflection,
An aimless actor portraying life.

Hang on.
When nothing is left,
Faith never abandons you.
Faith never deceives you.
Faith is the first and the last friend you will ever need.
Faith never charges or denies you.
Faith only requires you to believe.

Grab hold.
Don't deny your progress.
Your success is one decision away.

What choice is left—
Sorrow or strength,
Pain or relief,
Death or life reimagined,
Weakness or the will to fight?
You hold all the cards, make all the choices.
Show me your faith, and I will show you a new beginning.
Walk with me and see true strength—your power to overcome.
You will triumphantly conquer everything you put your mind to.
Walk in faith, or fall to failure.
You decide.

Faith Or Failure
10 Questions to Reflect On,

1. Can you recall a moment when believing in yourself helped you overcome a significant challenge?
    - What inner strength or mindset did you tap into, and how can you harness that again in future challenges?
2. What are the "darkest storms" in your life, and how have you navigated through them?
    - What specific coping mechanisms or sources of support have helped you weather these storms?
3. In what ways do you think self-belief has shaped your path or influenced your decisions?
    - How has your belief in yourself impacted not only your successes but also your ability to recover from setbacks?
4. How can you cultivate a stronger sense of faith in yourself during times of doubt?
    - What practices or affirmations could reinforce your self-confidence when faced with uncertainty?
5. What practical steps can you take to reinforce your resilience when facing failure?
    - What lessons from past failures can serve as tools for strengthening your ability to bounce back?
6. How do you see your personal growth affecting others around you?
    - In what ways can your journey of self-belief and resilience inspire or positively influence those in your life?

7. What legacy of resilience do you hope to leave behind?
    - How can your story of perseverance and faith in yourself serve as an example for future generations?
8. Can you identify a recent situation where you might have benefited from a stronger belief in your abilities?
    - What could have changed if you had acted from a place of confidence, and how will you approach similar situations differently next time?
9. How does this quote inspire you to act differently in your future endeavors?
    - What specific actions or changes will you implement to live in alignment with the power of faith over fear?
10. What specific qualities do you think embody the "true power" mentioned in the quote, and how can you develop them further?
    - What daily practices or habits can help you strengthen these qualities in your life?

Chapter 3: Follower or Leader

In today's society, we often find ourselves conforming to the opinions and expectations of others, following the crowd even when deep down we know we should be pursuing our own path. There are fleeting moments of independence, times when we feel free to make our own decisions, but the pressure to fit in and be accepted can pull us back into the tide of conformity. Acceptance feels comforting, like a warm blanket of approval, and it's easy to lose ourselves in the opinions of others. Being a follower can seem easier—there's less risk, less responsibility—but with it comes a sense of emptiness, as if we are living someone else's life instead of our own.

However, the weight of being a leader in our own lives, though difficult, is ultimately far more fulfilling. It requires strength and courage to step away from the crowd, to define our own values and beliefs, and to live authentically. The journey is often lonely, but it leads to a deeper sense of self-worth and purpose. True relationships—those where people accept you for who you really are— become invaluable. These connections, built on genuine friendship, are the ones that stand strong when you choose not to follow the crowd. They remind us that being accepted for our true selves is worth far more than blending into the masses. In these moments of clarity, we realize the profound importance of surrounding ourselves with people who see us, value us, and support our individuality.

The End Is The Beginning

"Once cloaked in the unremarkable, gray of the crowd, I followed paths, paved by the footsteps of others, A mere shadow among shadows, my doubts as heavy as the wool that blanketed my spirit. But within me, an ember of defiance glowed, undimmed by the conformity that surrounded it. In the crucible of self reflection, that ember sparked into a blaze, forging my transformation. Now, like a phoenix risen from the ashes of my own fears, I stand a glow with purpose and conviction. A leader, sculpted by the fierce flames of self belief, ready to illuminate new paths, not just for myself, but for all who seek light beyond the gray."

—Unknown

The End Is The Beginning

As the story unfolds and the truth becomes more distant,
The veil of trickery shudders among the lost, left shadowed.
The kings and their masters sit on high,
As the lost have no choice but to follow and abide.

The pendulum circles with no direction and no force—
Only a never-ending circle generating complacency.
The gifts continue to be given and received,
As a sea of servants are filled with emptiness, gratefully.

On a mountain of promises flows a river of lies.
Navigating the current, competition breeds hate.
Red, black, green, blue—the colors bleed together.
All that is left is the deception its offer implies.

As stress looms,
Visions are applied.
Hatred is fueled—
Let me out and free me,
Separate me from the separated,
Forgotten and left needing,
All the same in the blight of shame.

Eyes rage with burning fury,
Buried deep within the lost moments.
No words left,
Remembering days past punishments.

Without risk, we remain the same.

As we rise from the darkness,
Falling,
Holding on, losing grip.
Strength hidden in weakness,
An outsider watching and waiting—
A follower, a leader, a motivator, a coward.

How much is enough?
Powerless and left wanting,
Belly full, soul empty,
Shamelessly accepting a predetermined fate.

What do you really believe in?
Get off your knees and reach for the sky.
Time stops once the choice is made.
One voice spawns judgement—
We are the instrument where truth is weighed.

Until we discharge the thieves that control
And see the specters for who they are,
Tattered souvenirs of promises gone dry,
The sun fades and the darkness unfolds—
Finally understanding our freedom is denied.

The End Is The Beginning
10 Questions to Reflect On,

1. What aspects of conformity have you found yourself adhering to, and how have they affected your sense of self?
   - How can you begin to break free from these patterns of conformity to live a more authentic and purposeful life?
2. Can you identify a moment when you felt like merely a follower, lost in the crowd? What sparked the realization?
   - What did this experience teach you about the importance of individuality and forging your own path?
3. What doubts or fears have weighed you down the most, and how have you addressed them?
   - What strategies have helped you overcome these fears, and how can you continue to rise above them?
4. Reflect on the "ember of defiance" within you. What form does it take, and how has it manifested in your actions or decisions?
   - How has this defiance helped shape your character, and in what ways has it challenged the status quo?
5. How has the process of self-reflection contributed to your personal growth and transformation?
   - What specific moments of introspection have led to pivotal changes in your mindset or behavior?
6. In what ways have you experienced a metaphorical rebirth in your personal or professional life?

- What key moments or decisions have marked new beginnings, and how have they redefined your sense of purpose?

7. What characteristics do you believe define a true leader, and how do you embody these characteristics?
    - How can you further cultivate these qualities to guide others while staying true to your values?

8. How has taking on a leadership role, either by choice or circumstance, changed your relationships and interactions with others?
    - What lessons have you learned about balancing leadership with empathy and collaboration?

9. What new paths are you inspired to illuminate, and what steps are you taking to lead others towards them?
    - How do you envision using your experiences to create positive change in the lives of others?

10. Looking ahead, what future transformations do you aspire to achieve, and what challenges do you anticipate facing on this journey?
    - What personal growth or leadership goals are you setting for yourself, and how do you plan to overcome the obstacles in your way?

Chapter 4: Drained

Life has a way of draining us, slowly and relentlessly, as we juggle work, family, friends, and endless responsibilities. The demands pile up—each task, each commitment taking another piece of our energy. We push ourselves day after day, trying to meet expectations, maintain relationships, and keep everything afloat. Whether it's the pressure of a demanding job, the needs of family, or the constant presence of social obligations, it can feel like we are carrying a weight that never lifts. Over time, the exhaustion builds—mentally and physically—until we reach a point where it feels like we have nothing left to give. It's a deep exhaustion that clouds our mind and seeps into our bones, making even the smallest task seem insurmountable. We feel drained, as if life has stripped us of our strength and left us running on empty.

Yet, even in our most exhausted state, we know we cannot give up. Giving up simply isn't an option, because the world keeps moving and so must we. Responsibilities don't vanish because we're tired; there are people relying on us— family, friends, and even ourselves. It's this knowledge that pushes us forward when we feel like we have nothing left. There's a resilience within us, a flicker of strength that refuses to be extinguished, even when our minds and bodies are screaming for rest. In these moments, we discover just how strong we can be, finding reserves of determination we didn't know existed. Though the struggle may be overwhelming, and the weight of life may seem unbearable, we press on. In doing so, we prove to ourselves that even in our lowest moments, we are capable of enduring and rising above the exhaustion.

Drained

"Even when the light inside me feels dim, and my body is weighed down by the exhaustion of life, my will and strength are the embers that refuse to die out. I may be drained, but I will keep going."

—Unknown

Drained

This pain is my little uncontrolled quarter,
Repressing pressure, a well never-ending.
Deeper, a fraying rope—
How can I constantly take more?

A dream of reprieve,
A break never given.
A cup with a hole,
Consciously turning, hurling shameless.

A sacrifice,
Keeping score,
Selfishly unpacking my karma.
Consequences are tremendous—
Life meant to thrive,
Doomed and disguised.

Countless excuses forgiven,
Intermission brooding,
Wasting away, endeavoring to fight decay.
How far we fall when our vision is truth believed.

When did I stop believing?
A champion transposed to the part of the villain,
Savoring the story of success.
Our story we deny and repress.
Where are the answers?
Do I even know the questions?
Lesson after lesson, a weapon,
Deceived and condoned.

What happened to the fire,

The cheers and accolades?
Inside I am dying,
Forgotten truth, confidence just a memory.

How long will I choose to stay frayed?
Set this image on fire.
Look at the world with dreaming eyes,
Shape your truth and find your faith.

Your burden isn't any more or less than anyone else's.
Your choices are rightly yours to choose.
Decisions are made within fear to gain access to truth.
Kindness and faith are a paramount blessing.

A comfort when no hope is left,
Strength comes from the deepest part of the well.
Sadness and desolation are the spark to light your soul—
Ignite that fire you always cherished.

Wait no longer for it to begin.
You are here now, present.
Comfort will turn to labor.
Happiness will morph into desolation.
Confidence will dissolve into irrelevance.
Be vulnerable to your shrine of importance.

Don't turn your back on cue.
Rise each day a ruthless warrior,
Fighting doubt, fear, and irrelevance.
You can carry so much more if you believe.
Burn the walls of doubt, walk through the smoke—
Higher and higher you will be cleansed.

You are the sum of all gifts given and offered.
Only you can complete that which is procrastinated.
Concerned?
It will pass.

Be wild and free to accept your ability to adapt.
All the strength you will ever need is already contained within you.
Dive into the well,
Accept the pain—don't wait.
Grab that rope.
It might be frayed, but the rope is still strong.
Climb out.
Freedom is calling you, embracing all—don't chase it.

Either adapt and survive, or wither away and die inside.

Drained

10 Questions to Reflect On,

1. What situations or challenges have recently made you feel like the light inside you is dimming?
    - How have these challenges affected your motivation, and what steps can you take to reignite your inner light?
2. How do you typically recognize when you're feeling overwhelmed or exhausted?
    - What physical, emotional, or mental signs do you notice, and how can you address them before burnout occurs?
3. In what ways do you find your will and strength acting like persistent embers?
    - What qualities or experiences keep your inner drive alive, even when the flame feels weak?
4. What strategies do you use to keep these embers alive, especially during tough times?
    - Which practices or habits have proven most effective in helping you maintain resilience?
5. How do you define your inner strength, and what does it mean to you to "keep going"?
    - What personal values or beliefs shape your understanding of perseverance and strength?
6. Can you think of a specific instance where you felt drained but continued to push through? What motivated you?

- What inner or external motivators helped you continue when you felt like giving up?
7. What lessons have you learned about yourself through these experiences of fatigue and perseverance?
    - How have these experiences helped you better understand your limits and your capacity for growth?
8. How do you balance the need to persist with the need to rest and recharge?
    - What methods do you use to ensure you don't push yourself too far, and how do you prioritize rest?
9. Who or what provides you with support or inspiration when you feel your energy waning?
    - How can you lean more on these sources of support when you need them most?
10. Looking forward, what steps can you take to better manage your energy and maintain your resilience?
    - What changes in routine or mindset can help you sustain your energy over the long term?

Chapter 5: Mirror

The way we see ourselves in the mirror holds incredible power. A mirror isn't just a collection of polished sand reflecting our image; it's a portal into our deepest thoughts and feelings—a window into either a bright and beautiful place of self acceptance or a dark abyss of sadness and deception. When we look at our reflection, we often focus on the flaws, on every imperfection that makes us feel inadequate. We pick apart the smallest details: how we're not attractive enough, not healthy enough, or not in the shape we want to be. But the reflection goes deeper than skin—it can reveal the masks we wear every day, the faces we present to the world that hide our true emotions. Sometimes, staring back at us is the storm of insecurity, calamity, or even self-deception, which threatens to destroy us from the inside out. The mirror can be a painful reminder of all that we feel we lack.

However, the mirror can also be a beautiful thing when we look through it with clear, non-judgmental eyes. It's important to recognize that no one is perfect, and that the person in the mirror is a work in progress, just like everyone else. Instead of pulling out the filtered flaws, we can choose to see the good, unfiltered qualities that make us who we are. The mirror reflects not just the imperfections but also the strength, the kindness, and the inner beauty we often overlook. We are more than the scars we hide behind masks—we are complex beings, full of both light and shadows. By embracing both, we can find a sense of peace in our reflection, knowing that what we see is not meant to be perfect, but real.

Mirror

"Looking in the mirror, you confront not the polished facade crafted for the world's gaze, but the unvarnished truth of who you are. It's a reflection stripped of pretense, revealing the quiet strength, the hidden scars, and the soul that longs to be seen, unmasked, unfiltered, undeniably real."

—Unknown

Mirror

Sprouting from the ground,
Fighting for every inch.
Light, surface, pieces of your soul.
I damned change—I am willing.

Reaching through—
No.
Shrinking down to its parts,
Pieces of growth that disassemble covertly.

Something holds you, binds you to its challenge.
Walls closing in, blind and broken.
It is automatic, willfully discharged as routine.
The relief never comes, failing to change when change is clear.

Don't fool yourself—you have already stopped believing.
Change's offers are finite.
Sitting in your disbelief, that the image you see in front of you
Has always been your answer.

The fear you carry is empty baggage,
Clutter contained in a full mind, wounded.
The image is the truth, not the illusion,
While the illusion is the ruler, chained.

Numerous lessons instructed,
Deemed worthless when casually dismissed.
What circumstances claim your attention,

Wasting your time, scarring the image you see?

Take away the faithless phase—
With casual actors portraying multiple faces,
Blissfully unaware of your ambition for growth.
Burnout, with collateral damage, self-inflicted.

This is who I am.
I have chosen to become this, not more.
Is there any reprieve?
Freedom reminisced.

Crawling as we fall,
Leaving it because it is too hard.
Looking up from the ground,
Remembering our deception is reason enough to fail.

Your reflection is clear—no lies, no pretense, only you looking back at you.
Look deep within—the truth is not a trick, it is a gamble full of risk.
Don't forsake the truth from you standing in your way.
Without risk, there is no reward.

Step through the visage—it requires courage.
The passage is full of fear, pain, broken dreams, lies, and loss.
Drag yourself up and wipe the dirt off—
Your strength will astound.

Grab hold.
You have taken your beating. They are only scars.
Your character—it's not too late. No more darkness, only light.
The door is open,

Cleansed of your reflection.
Fragmented.
No more hiding.
Look through your reflection—
See the real you in all your glory.
What is left is the only reality you will ever need.

Mirror

10 Questions to Reflect On,

1. What differences do you notice between the person you present to the world and the person you see in the mirror?
   - How do these differences affect your relationships, sense of self, or personal fulfillment?
2. What are some qualities you see in your reflection that you typically keep hidden from others?
   - What would it take for you to feel safe or confident enough to reveal these qualities?
3. Why might you feel the need to mask certain aspects of your true self?
   - What fears or insecurities drive this masking, and how can you begin to address them?
4. How does it feel to confront your unfiltered self in the mirror?
   - What emotions arise when you see yourself without pretense, and how do you manage those feelings?
5. What strengths do you observe in your true self that you might undervalue or overlook?
   - How can you cultivate greater awareness and appreciation for these strengths in your daily life?
6. Are there scars or vulnerabilities visible in the mirror that you feel need healing or acceptance?
   - What steps can you take to heal or embrace these parts of yourself with compassion and understanding?

7. How can embracing your reflection as it truly is impact your self-esteem and self-acceptance?
    - What practices or shifts in mindset could help you foster a deeper sense of self-love and authenticity?
8. What steps can you take to align the person you show to the world more closely with the person you see in the mirror?
    - How can you gradually let go of masks or facades to live a more integrated and genuine life?
9. How do your reflections on this quote change your perspective on authenticity and vulnerability?
    - What new insights or shifts in understanding have emerged from contemplating this quote?
10. What would you like to change about the way you see yourself in the mirror, if anything?
    - What inner work or external actions can help you achieve this change, or do you feel that acceptance is the key?

Chapter 6: As I Rise

Faith is a deeply personal journey, but it's also a universal experience. Whether through religion, spirituality, or simply a belief in something greater than ourselves, faith has the power to guide us through life's challenges. It teaches us that we are part of something bigger, something that connects us all—whether we call that force God, the universe, or something else entirely. While I personally dedicate my faith to the Lord Jesus Christ, I understand that not everyone subscribes to the same belief system. That's okay. Faith, in whatever form it takes, binds us together in the shared pursuit of meaning and purpose.

Believing in ourselves is crucial; it gives us the strength to pursue our dreams and overcome obstacles. But there is a higher power—something beyond our individual efforts—that grounds us and reminds us that we are not alone. This could be found in Catholicism, Judaism, Hinduism, Buddhism, Islam, or even in the principles of atheism that emphasize reason and morality. Whatever form faith takes, it helps us navigate the complexities of life, offering us hope, guidance, and a sense of connection to the world and people around us.

At the core, faith reminds us that nothing can create itself from nothing. If we accept this, then we acknowledge that something greater must have made us all. It's in this belief that we find purpose—whether we call it God, the universe, or another name—and it's this purpose that inspires us to keep striving to be the best people we can be. So, have faith. Believe in something more, and let that belief give you the strength to keep fighting the good fight, to grow, and to keep seeking the light, no matter the path you choose to follow.

As I Rise

"Each morning, I rise with a heart full of gratitude, thankful to God for the gift of life, the blessing of health, the joy of happiness, the abundance of prosperity, the warmth of friendships, and the strength of relationships. For every breath I take, I give thanks." —Unknown

As I Rise

Thank you, Lord, for letting me rise another day to see all the beauty you have made.

Thank you, Lord, for giving me your forgiveness—
That I might not deserve, but you offer me just the same.

Thank you, Lord, for giving me your gifts of health, family, and friends,
Those that share with me friendship, love, and strength,
So I know the true value of life.

Thank you, Lord, for showing me that when I rise another day,
I can make a difference in someone's life—
Be the rock they need, a word of encouragement,
And a constant reminder of your love.

Thank you, Lord, for showing me strength when I have none,
Faith in myself when my faith has run out,
And confidence to go on when I fear I have nothing left to fight for.

Thank you, Lord, for showing me your grace,
For without it, I am unable to see the light.

Thank you, Lord, for letting me rise with faithful hopes and dreams for the world,
To see all its beauty through fresh eyes.

Finally, as I rise, thank you, Lord, for the love you give me each day.
As my eyes wake to first light,
I become a better person without fear of death—

A man with strength of purpose, driven
To fight every single day in your name. Amen.

As I Rise
10 Questions to Reflect On,

1. What am I most grateful for in my life today?
    - How does focusing on gratitude change my mindset and outlook for the day?
2. How has God blessed me with health and strength?
    - How can I use my health and strength to positively impact others?
3. Who are the people in my life that bring me love and joy?
    - How can I express my appreciation for these people today?
4. What relationships am I thankful for, and how can I nurture them today?
    - What small actions can I take to strengthen these relationships?
5. What opportunities do I have today to grow and prosper?
    - How can I make the most of these opportunities, both big and small?
6. How has God provided for my needs, and how can I show appreciation?
    - In what ways can I share my blessings with others to show my gratitude?
7. What moments of happiness did I experience recently, and how can I create more?
    - How can I focus on creating joy in the simple moments of life?

8. What challenges have I overcome with God's help, and what can I learn from them?
    - How can I apply those lessons to future obstacles I might face?
9. How can I use my gifts and talents to serve others today?
    - What specific actions can I take to make a difference in someone's life today?
10. What small, everyday blessings am I overlooking, and how can I be more mindful of them?
    - How can I practice mindfulness to appreciate the beauty in the little things?

Chapter 7: Infidelity

Temptation in relationships is a powerful force, capable of creeping in when least expected, slowly eroding the trust that once seemed unbreakable. Infidelity doesn't happen in a moment—it builds from seemingly harmless thoughts, from justifications we create to ease our conscience. We begin to fabricate excuses, convincing ourselves that our actions are justified: "It's just a distraction," "They'll never know," or "Things aren't the same as they used to be." But with each step toward betrayal, we lose sight of the commitment we made to our significant other —the promise to honor, love, and protect the bond that unites us. The moment we give in to temptation, trust shatters, and what was once solid crumbles into doubt and betrayal.

The damage caused by infidelity runs deep, not only destroying our own sense of self but also harming the ones we love. The relationship that once provided security and warmth is left in ruins, and the emotional toll can leave lasting scars. The one who was betrayed often suffers in silence, questioning their worth, replaying moments of doubt, and feeling the sharp sting of broken trust. But the harm extends beyond just the two people involved—it touches family, friends, and even future relationships. Learning that commitment is more than just a word but the very foundation of love is essential. It's a constant effort to uphold the promise made, to resist temptation, and to cherish the bond above fleeting desires. In the end, succumbing to temptation destroys far more than the relationship—it tears apart the integrity and love we once took for granted.

Confessions Of A Madman

"Temptation lures with a sweet taste, but the bitter price is paid in shattered trust, lingering guilt, and the eternal ache of love betrayed. In the end, the truth we hide becomes the chains that bind us, while the decisions we make carve the path of our own undoing." — Unknown

Confessions of a Madman

I have committed many sins,
And in this, I feel no remorse.
My feelings are justified—
Pain from a negligent source.

The molding of forbidden fruit,
A taste too sweet to deny.
Hidden strength, focused desire,
Lies concealed within a lie.

The union of the joining,
Happiness up for sale.
Variety is a reward—
Relations are doomed to fail.

We met in our youth,
Ideas were new and fresh.
Love, to us, was complete,
Sharing of our minds,
The joining of the flesh.

Complacency came easy,
But it all remained the same.
Love was never in question,
Yet routine still remained.

Is not desire and hunger
Imbued for all time?

Searching for the unknown,
One is always left behind.

Wandering aimlessly through emptiness,
Seeking to fill the void,
Only the one you're with can't offer
That which has been destroyed.

Situations are fleeting,
The conscious mind will wander.
Judgment will come,
Soulless and encumbered.

One loves the feeling,
The rush that it brings.
The other fears the conflict
And the pain that it stings.

Power is predetermined,
Choices are made.
The costs are overlooked,
Yet the price must be paid.

One locked in torment,
Another so alone.
Interrupted loyalty—
Someone must atone.

Jealous accusations,
Powerless to hide.
Guilt resides in silence,
Our conscience will decide.

A tragedy proclaimed,
Words from a mendacious ghost.
A rampant influx of malice—
A weak defense at most.

One has made a decision,
Constructing what's left.
As love disappears,
When one's honor is not kept.

Your decision must be made—
To resist would be the choice.
Hiding from the truth
Destroys love's silent voice.

The thought of missing out
Begins when newness fades.
As with love, feelings are eternal,
Leaving sins for you to contemplate.

Some problems will arise,
One might wish to stray.
Choices must be made—
Heed caution on your way.

A vile perpetrator of deceit,
One weak to flesh's taste.
The journey of relationships' infinite circle
Will forever be defaced.

The excuses will continue—
A coward you will become.

The truth will be the ending,
A self-governing axiom.

If truth is your choice,
You will be met with disdain.
Remember, love will never be mended
If you won't embrace the pain.

If you choose to keep the secret,
The mark will be seen by all.
No matter how well you guard it,
The guilt will force its fall.

A final stand must be taken—
The choice of time is yours.
Remember, love's offer is fleeting
When your heart takes dishonest detours.

Confessions Of A Madman
10 Questions to Reflect On,

1. What temptations in my life have led me away from my true values?
   - Reflect on moments where desires have clouded your judgment.
2. How have I justified actions that I knew were wrong?
   - Consider the ways you've rationalized choices that conflicted with your morals.
3. What are the long-term consequences of my decisions on those I care about?
   - Think about how your actions have impacted relationships and trust.
4. In what ways have I allowed fear to silence my truth?
   - Explore moments where fear prevented you from being honest, both with yourself and others.
5. How has routine and complacency affected my relationships?
   - Reflect on how falling into patterns may have dulled the connection with others.
6. What unresolved guilt do I carry, and how is it affecting my present?
   - Examine the weight of past actions and how they continue to influence your life.
7. Where in my life am I avoiding difficult truths?
   - Identify areas where you might be hiding from reality or avoiding necessary confrontations.
8. How do I handle the balance between desire and commitment?

- Consider how you manage personal desires in the context of commitments to others.

9. What steps can I take to rebuild trust, either with myself or others?
    - Think about what actions you can take to restore integrity and trust in relationships.

10. How can I ensure that my future decisions align with my core values?
    - Reflect on how to stay true to your beliefs and principles moving forward.

Chapter 8: Resilience

Reaching our true potential in life is an incredibly difficult journey, fraught with inner conflicts and shaped by both internal and external influences. We battle against our own fears, doubts, and insecurities, while simultaneously dealing with the pressures and expectations of the world around us. These forces often cloud our vision and affect our ability to achieve personal goals—those things that truly fulfill us. Fear, in particular, becomes a powerful barrier, keeping us from stepping into our full potential. We allow it to control our actions and choices, painting distorted pictures of who we are and what we are capable of. These images are reinforced by the deceptions we tell ourselves: that we aren't good enough, that we'll fail, or that we don't deserve success. Such thoughts can sabotage our efforts, making it harder to move forward and realize our ambitions.

In life, there must be balance, but with balance comes uncertainty, especially when we try to control outcomes that are beyond our grasp. Our past experiences are a double-edged sword—they serve as a wellspring of wisdom, teaching us valuable lessons, but they can also hold us back. If we fall into patterns of repeating the same mistakes or allowing past failures to dictate our future, we create more setbacks that prevent us from attaining our goals. To reach the pinnacle of life, we must constantly reflect, learn, and move forward in a steady, purposeful way. It requires redefining and reinforcing our character, learning from both our successes and failures. By embracing this process of growth and self-discovery, we can gradually break free from the chains of fear and deception, allowing ourselves to rise toward the potential we were meant to fulfill.

Pinnacle

"Embark on a journey through the tempest of the mind, where chaos and clarity intertwine. In the shadows of self-doubt and the peaks of realization, discover the strength to rise above your own fears and embrace the pinnacle of your true self." — Unknown

Pinnacle

Let the mystery live,
Calling unto itself. Hidden,
Deceived, Devised,
Willing to its madness.

Civil on both sides,
Nothing but a shadow,
Fulfilled by itself,
Except from its completion.

Growth from a cowardly stance,
Viewed from a tainted yet somber impression.
Realization complacent with nothing,
Except from its idle uncertainty.

Redefine its coercion,
Falsely creating a symbiotic connection,
Using its simplistic organized theme,
Scarring any advance yet to be contained.

The tempest has no name,
Traveling on the wings of your sanity,
Draining a seemingly singular existence,
Hidden in reality where cooperation is made.

A race has started,
Contained within the mind's infinite complexity,
Suggesting a competition of one's duality,

Residing in a role falsely made.

Moments lived are residual—
Past triumphs and transgressions take hold.
Reliance on your denial—
Life events will be shrouded,
Feeling falseness, controlled.

Tremble, for the fear resides in you.
Saint or sinner, unclean on the whole,
Separate from this, climbing high.
Reach out for understanding—
Pain is returned.
Push through, retain something,
Remembering nothing.

Ideally, we choose a path,
A path undecided unto you.
Construction for an explanation,
Resulting in desperation.

You have resolved a path at this point,
A peak too high, limiting perhaps.
Watch as it passes,
Too afraid to move,
Too terrified to believe.

Jumble your thoughts,
Your mind can be unforgiving.
Left at an impasse,
Redefining your purpose in living.

I simply cannot control the unknown,
But within my personal chaos,
Within chaos, I find my wealth—
Wealth within time,
Time uncontrolled by self.

I happened upon my view,
This all-encompassing deception that I believe to be me.
Then I fall back, return with empty glances—
A mistaken fool who was offered too many chances.

I have traveled many roads
And found that I continue the same game.
I am unfocused and fallible—
No matter how hard I try,
I still remain the same.

So left alone I am to decide,
Daring to dream on my own,
Without the false illuminations I set upon myself,
Knowing that I am incomplete.
I would choose to rise to life's pinnacle and finally live again.

Pinnacle

10 Questions to Reflect On,

1. What internal struggles have I been avoiding, and how do they shape my actions?
   - Consider the inner conflicts that influence your decisions and behaviors.
2. How do I define my own 'pinnacle,' and what does it mean to truly reach it?
   - Reflect on your personal goals and what success or fulfillment looks like for you.
3. In what ways have I allowed fear to prevent me from pursuing my true potential?
   - Examine the fears that hold you back from achieving your aspirations.
4. How has chaos played a role in my life, and what have I learned from it?
   - Think about moments of disorder and confusion and how they've contributed to your growth.
5. What false beliefs about myself do I need to let go of to move forward?
   - Identify limiting beliefs or self-deceptions that hinder your progress.
6. How do I balance the desire for control with the acceptance of uncertainty?

- Explore the tension between trying to control outcomes and embracing the unknown.

7. What past experiences continue to shape my present decisions, for better or worse?
    - Reflect on how past triumphs and mistakes influence your current path.

8. In what ways can I redefine my purpose to align more closely with my true self?
    - Consider how you might adjust your goals or values to better reflect who you are.

9. How do I respond to setbacks, and what do they reveal about my character?
    - Think about your reactions to challenges and what they say about your resilience and growth.

10. What steps can I take today to begin rising towards my own pinnacle?
    - Reflect on actionable steps you can take to start moving toward your highest potential.

Chapter 9: Change

Change is a constant in our lives, something we all desire, yet something we often struggle with. It touches every part of our existence—work, home, family, and relationships—each of which brings its own challenges. External change, while often difficult, tends to be more manageable because it is outside of our control. We adapt to new circumstances, changes in our environment, or shifts in relationships, knowing that we must cope with the hand we've been dealt. But it is personal change, the kind that requires deep introspection and effort, that is often the hardest to face. Whether it's a habit, a way of thinking, or even how we feel about a person, place, or subject, these ingrained aspects of ourselves— often rooted in childhood or long-held beliefs—become the hardest barriers to overcome.

When it comes to personal change, we often fail because it requires not only effort but also a conscious choice to transform something internal. The difficulty lies in breaking away from patterns and routines that feel familiar, even when they no longer serve us. It's easy to slip back into old ways because they're comfortable, and the road to change feels lonely and uncertain. However, real change begins when we make the choice to take control of our personal growth. It's in this conscious decision that we can begin to command change, to grow from the inside out. And though the path is not always easy, we must remember that failure is not the end. If we fall, we stand up and try again. If the change is meaningful to us, we will find the strength and willpower within to achieve it. True transformation comes from perseverance, from knowing that despite setbacks, the desire to evolve and become a better version of ourselves is worth the effort.

The Lonely Road Of Change

"Change is not something we wait for; it is something we must choose. Growth begins the moment we decide to step away from what holds us back and move toward what we are meant to become."

— Unknown

The Lonely Road of Change

To look into the eyes of destiny,
One must focus on the truth—
A truth hidden from searching eyes,
Where words are written in an empty book.

You stand alone,
Feeling your grip held tight.
But this false sheath drowns you,
Depleting your strength each night.

Sad though it may seem,
You move on as if it will pass.
Until you face your fears,
It will ceaselessly last.

The choice is not clear,
It is not yet time to let die
All the useless dwelling
You've learned to rely on, deep inside.

The decision to change,
The decision to grow,
The decision to rise above,
The decision to let go.

Silent contemplation—
Free from distraction,
For quiet noise clouds your judgment,

Leading to unwanted reaction.

The lonely road of change
Begins with untrained steps.
Command nothing in haste,
Discern each thought with deliberate care.

The decision to change,
The decision to grow,
The decision to rise above,
The decision to grant control.

Change is decision,
And decision is change.
Motivate yourself,
Broaden your range.

Some will say,
"Change cannot take place.
Once steps are taken,
They can never be retraced."

I say they are wrong.

Change is a state of mind.
Choose a new direction,
And change is what you will find.

Listen—
It has spoken to you.
A decision will come,
What will you do?

If you feel it is out of reach,
And you can go no further,
Look at yourself.
Find the will to be stronger.

The decision to change,
The decision to grow,
The decision to rise above,
The decision to take control.

Be a better person,
For change begins within.
New feelings will come,
Expanding your range again.

Don't try to change others.
Change must start inside you.
Every change has a beginning,
And it starts in your heart,
Where you must decide what's true.

Don't change just to please others.
You are free to choose your own way.
Understand, change can be deceptive,
And those around you may fade away.

Change is not easy,
Routine feels safe.
But change brings new outcomes,
If you truly believe in its grace.

Age brings choices,
Time brings regret.
Progress is missed,
When past voices are left unchecked.

If change is needed,
Let the decision be true.
All hope comes from this,
But beware of moving too soon.

They say, "Paint a leopard, and the spots remain."
But beneath the paint, the spots have changed.
How is there change?

Change comes from action in decision.
When you choose to change, good or bad,
You have altered your path.
Keep that change, and you've created new spots,
A new self, where nothing is set in stone.
Learn this—there's nothing you cannot do,
If you truly decide to change your life.

Enjoy your life,

The Lonely Road Of Change
10 Questions to Reflect On,

1. What truths about myself have I been avoiding, and how can I confront them?
   - Consider the hidden truths that may be affecting your ability to grow.

2. What is currently holding me back from embracing change?
   - Identify the fears, habits, or circumstances that are preventing you from moving forward.

3. How can I let go of the past and stop relying on old patterns of thought?
   - Reflect on ways to break free from routines or mindsets that no longer serve you.

4. What areas of my life need growth, and what steps can I take to start that process?
   - Explore the parts of your life that could benefit from intentional development.

5. When have I been hesitant to make a change, and what were the consequences?
   - Think about times you resisted change and the impact it had on your life.

6. What role does fear play in my decision-making process?
   - Reflect on how fear influences your choices and your willingness to take risks.

7. How can I practice self-motivation and take control of my personal growth?
    - Consider how you can become more proactive in fostering change.
8. What distractions in my life cloud my judgment, and how can I clear them?
    - Identify the noise or distractions that prevent you from focusing on meaningful decisions.
9. How can I better embrace the uncertainty that comes with change?
    - Reflect on how you deal with uncertainty and how you can become more comfortable with it.
10. What is one change I can make today that will positively impact my future?
    - Think of a single, actionable step you can take now to set yourself on a path of growth.

Chapter 10: Life Is The Secret

The secret of life, often elusive, lies in the very act of living itself. We spend so much time searching for meaning, chasing after goals, and grappling with our place in the world that we forget the truth right before us: life is the secret. It's only when we approach the end of our journey that the veil lifts, revealing that the beauty was in the experiences, the mysteries, the friendships, the family, and the love we've encountered along the way. Yet, life has a dual nature. Alongside its brightness, there are shadows—regrets that gnaw at us, moments when we stand on the edge, staring into the abyss of our reality. Sometimes, the life we live doesn't match the life we dreamed, and that realization can be painful.

Even in the darkest times, though, the secret of life remains: it is living. Life itself, with all its complexities, is a gift more precious than we often realize. Each day offers a chance to embrace its vibrancy, to wake with purpose, and to absorb the beauty all around us. The key is to face life without clinging to regrets, to release the darkness that threatens to cloud our vision. In doing so, we learn to live the secret, appreciating the journey in all its forms, both joyful and challenging, as the most profound experience we are ever given.

The Secret

"Life's true secret isn't hidden—it's the very act of living it fully. The vibrant side of life is filled with beauty, joy, and color, while the darker side of regret looms when we fail to embrace it. Only when we stand at the edge, gazing back at what was left unlived, do we realize the precious gift we've been given. Don't wait until it's too late to choose the vibrant path."

—Unknown

The Secret

What is it?
This gift we wish to attain—
Grains of sand through time,
A privilege captured following a smile.
Feeling, energy, vitality, vigor, strength, and peace—
A prerequisite for concession,
Seconds of eternity,
Empty and passed up by preference.

We face the morning,
Never truly knowing its grace,
Ardently searching for the clues
Hidden by a mist—timeless, ageless, and abiding.

A rhythm that resonates as it's confused—
The same old distraction, a conscript enrolled to serve.
Cheers, a toast to all, and to all unite—
An assemblage of puppets,
None knowing its secret.

The secret is implied when we are young,
Through eyes that see the grace and beauty the gift contains.
Distraction offers thundering attraction to help us forget.
It calls us,
Failing to break through—
Adamant and insurgent.

The trade-off is the truth—
Everything we have ever wanted and accepted as significant,
Furthest from the answer we could possibly be.
The assurance of safety as a certainty,
Never seeing the answer is right in front of you all the time.

The secret returns when we are very old,
Wise in the ways of the world,
Ignorant of the truth that the secret has roared.
Only at the end of our journey,
Ultimately, the secret is revealed.

How precious is this life that has been granted to us—
Forgetting all the little things that have been molded and grown.
We manifest an unmistakable presence.
Material matters not, substance speaks—are we listening?

Every experience,
Every reaction,
Every interaction,
Every lesson,
Every heartbeat—
Respectively, everything.

Our life is the mystery,
The gift that screams with all resound.
Cherish it, nurture it,
Never take it for granted.
Only offered once,
Removed in the blink of an eye.
Don't chase it, embrace it.

Be the light of your life and let your light shine.
Steal that light and share it with the world.
You are that secret—
Everything you are.
God's gift.
Simply put, you are amazing!

The Secret

10 Questions to Reflect On,

1. Am I fully embracing the vibrant side of life, or am I letting fear hold me back?
    - What fears are preventing me from living more fully, and how can I confront them?
2. What areas of my life are filled with color and joy, and how can I cultivate more of them?
    - How can I dedicate more time to the things and people that bring me the most joy?
3. Where in my life am I experiencing regret, and how can I begin to heal from it?
    - What steps can I take to forgive myself and move forward from this regret?
4. Am I living each day with purpose, or am I allowing time to slip by unnoticed?
    - How can I refocus my energy to make each day more meaningful?
5. How can I better appreciate the beauty in the everyday moments of my life?
    - What daily practices can I incorporate to remind myself to be more present?
6. What opportunities have I missed, and how can I avoid future regrets?
    - How can I become more proactive in recognizing and seizing opportunities?
7. Am I making choices that align with living a full and vibrant life?

- What adjustments can I make to ensure my choices reflect my desire for a meaningful life?

8. How do I confront the darker sides of my past without letting them define my future?
    - What lessons can I take from my past, and how can I use them to shape a better future?

9. What small steps can I take today to move toward a life of no regrets?
    - What is one actionable goal I can start today that will bring me closer to my ideal life?

10. How can I ensure that when I look back on my life, I see more vibrancy than darkness?
    - How can I build a life filled with more positive experiences and fewer missed opportunities?

Chapter 11: Prison Of Yesterday

Living a life within the past is like residing in a self-made prison, one built from regrets and missed opportunities. We often get trapped, haunted by what we should have done, failing to acknowledge all that we have done. The weight of past mistakes chains us to a life of repetition, moving like drones through the motions, our once grand dreams dissolving in the shadows of fear and hesitation. Time and excuses become crutches, something to lean on rather than tools to break free. Decisions shaped by the past begin to entrap us, stripping away the freedom we once had to forge a new path. Living in the shadows of yesterday, we lose sight of today's possibilities, and with them, our future.

The prison of yesterday is just that—a prison. When we cling to the past rather than learn from it, we remain confined, unable to move forward. Life's lessons are meant to guide us, not hold us back. While happy memories can make us smile, the darker ones, if not faced and understood, doom us to repeat the same mistakes. Stepping over the barriers of regret means reclaiming your freedom, breaking away from the patterns of yesterday to walk toward the future. It's there, beyond the bars of the past, where your true freedom awaits, and with it, the chance to fully live.

Signs

"In the quiet moments of deep reflection, I see the shadows of my past and the bright signs of my future. Bound by the prison of yesterday, I now realize that the key to my freedom has always been in front of me—everything I need to know is within reach, waiting for me to embrace it."

—Unknown

Signs

The signs have been compiling
As we pass through all the things we should have done,
Finding out all the things we could have done
Were the limits we placed but never returned to revise.

Your nature is a lesson that we all learned,
Never realizing the overload was the change pleaded.
Trying to teach a life removed of repetition and constancy
Is a field of fire, burning out of control, settling for the damage.

More than you can handle—
Big dreams,
Wishes dissolved and chased.
Sleeping, never seeing what your blindness has been tracing.

Time discovers you and reminds you—
A breeze blowing, escaping the pause, the silence of peace.
Falling short, past the blinders, disillusion, and small reminders—
A flashback of suspicious signs, hollow and hopeless.

Learning how to step outside yourself,
Proudly accepting failure, fighting for what matters.
Pushing away the self-doubt, pain, and suddenness,
Accepting a peace well deserved.

Walls closing in, designed to defeat.
The toll rises—prices are too high to recover.

Set yourself free.
Your nightfall isn't an ending.
Falling apart—
The pieces fit together:
Excuses,
Responses.

Don't dismiss the future when your prison is your past.
Admit when you have nothing left—
The well is never truly empty,
With strength only you can surpass.

Leave behind the old limitations,
Never forgetting the shell of knowledge unbalanced.
Listen to your resolve and revolt—
You get a second chance, follow the signs.
Don't waste the gift you have been given.
Do better!

Signs
10 Questions to Reflect On,

1. What specific shadows from your past do you see in moments of deep reflection?
   - How do these memories shape the way you view yourself today?
2. How do these shadows affect your daily life and decisions?
   - What recurring patterns or behaviors stem from these past experiences?
3. What are the "bright signs" of your future that you envision?
   - How can you focus on these positive signs to motivate your actions?
4. In what ways do you feel bound by the past, and how does this affect your sense of freedom?
   - What specific events or beliefs keep you tethered to your past?
5. What does the key to your freedom look like in practical terms?
   - How can you begin to unlock this freedom in small, manageable ways?
6. How can you actively work to free yourself from the "prison of yesterday"?
   - What is one practical step you can take today to release the grip of the past?
7. What steps can you take to embrace the knowledge and tools that are within your reach?

- How can you better use your existing skills and resources to move forward?

8. How has your perspective on your potential and capabilities evolved over time?
    - What pivotal moments have contributed to your growth and self-belief?

9. What barriers must you overcome to fully embrace your future?
    - Are these barriers internal (self-doubt) or external (circumstances), and how can you overcome them?

10. What will be your first step towards utilizing the key to your freedom?
    - How can you commit to taking this first step today?

Chapter 12: Friend or Fair Weather

True friendship is a bond that transcends time, distance, and circumstance, built on a foundation of character, mutual respect, loyalty, honesty, and care. It's the kind of friendship that stands unwavering through the highs and lows of life, offering a steady hand in times of need and sharing in the joy of successes without a trace of envy. True friends are those who see you for who you are, flaws and all, and still stand by your side, supporting your growth and challenging you to be the best version of yourself. They are the ones who listen without judgment, speak with honesty even when the truth is hard to hear, and show up not just when it's convenient, but when it truly matters. In the deepest valleys of life, these friends are your strength, never hesitating to shoulder some of the burden, because their care for you is unconditional and everlasting.

On the other hand, a "fair-weather friend" is the antithesis of this enduring bond. They are present when it benefits them, offering friendship only on a superficial level or when things are going well. Their loyalty is conditional, their support fleeting, and their motives often self-serving. When the storms of life come, they vanish, leaving you to weather the turbulence alone. These friends may offer smiles and good times on the surface, but they lack the depth of true connection. In this journey through life, it's important to recognize that true friendships are rare gems, and we should consider ourselves lucky to have even four or five such friends. Acquaintances may come and go, but the few who offer unwavering loyalty and care are the ones who make life richer, and those bonds are worth cherishing and holding onto.

Yes

"Standing between the warmth of genuine friendship and the cold indifference of selfishness, I find myself at a crossroads. On one side, the true friend radiates loyalty, care, and unwavering support, a beacon of light in my life. On the other, the fair-weather friend lingers in the shadows, their presence only felt when there is something to gain, their affection fleeting and conditional. In this moment of clarity, I understand that true bonds are not built on convenience or self-interest but are nurtured in the enduring glow of selflessness and mutual respect." —Unknown

Yes

The anger is momentous and is calling out to me.
The sounds are focused on certain abstract feelings.
They are given only to those who have finally passed—
Passed into the dwelling of denial.

Return it to the direction least traveled.
It's all or nothing,
Lost within its deception of radical thought,
Focused on feeling its offering,
Then expending all of your energy hiding it,
Finally forgetting the reasons for everything.

You cherish the friendships, and forget the reasons.
You sacrifice all for that aim,
Turning it all around, no matter the cost,
Leaving nothing left that could ever be the same.

The thoughts of perfection within that friendship
Can only be claimed by a soul-less person—
Willfully and completely denying all reason
To be true to the nature of honor.

To take control can only mean loss.
To take advantage—can one attain?
Judging not on the individual or their character,
But only on the reality of its heaven
And your intervention within their life.

Should one meddle with the rules of friendship?
Should one dictate its soul-less justification?
Can it be completely true to its own personal nature—
A nature that has been written and re-written over and over again?

It's simply conjecture.
One will banter back and forth.
Maybe I should have seen it a long time ago,
Helpless, getting through it—
Walking alone in a world full of friends,
Only descending deeper into the void of divinity.

Sending out a message, saving all for none or nothing,
Hearing with clogged thought,
Salable and fallible,
Undeniably alone.
Once true in nature,
One will outlast and overcome—
Searching, wanting, and waiting patiently
For a hint of what we have hidden from.

I should have seen it a long time ago,
Seen it coming
As I have listened—
Hearing the mass of noises,
Clouding my reason.
They all have walked by,
Out the door of my life,
Returning only in times of their need.

Have I breathed?
Have I shared my breath?
Have I burdened my soul
To be that friend?

Something reminds me,
Recalling lasting occasions,
Engrained in my freedom,
Mortally wounding me.

Alas, I come back to my space,
Comfort from my retreat,
Allowing false character,
A wanton destruction—
The consolation is complete.

I can only smile and believe I am lasting,
Truthful unto myself and my feelings.
I can't deny what I remember,
I can only forget the area I placed it.

I stand there with you,
I will grow with you.
I will be all that I am—
That is enough,
Enough for both of us.
Growing together,
Understanding each other,
Guiding you as you walk away.

The friend you have, now wordless,
Speaks to you through action—

The action that can only be lasting,
One day causing you to believe in your friendless reaction.

Yes

10 Questions to Reflect On,

1. Which of my friendships are built on mutual respect, loyalty, and genuine care?
   - What actions or behaviors demonstrate these values in my relationships, and how do I reciprocate them?
2. How do I differentiate between a true friend and a fair-weather friend in my life?
   - What specific patterns of behavior or circumstances reveal someone's true loyalty or reveal their self-interest?
3. Am I offering the same level of support and selflessness to my friends that I seek from them?
   - In what ways could I improve my actions to ensure I am meeting my friends' emotional needs without expecting something in return?
4. Are there relationships in my life where the connection feels one-sided or conditional?
   - What boundaries or conversations could help balance these relationships, or is it time to let them go?
5. How can I better recognize when someone is only present for their own benefit?
   - What signs have I overlooked in the past, and how can I develop better awareness to protect myself emotionally in the future?
6. What qualities do I value most in a friend, and how do those align with my current relationships?

- How do my friends' actions reflect the qualities I value, and are there areas where compromise or growth is necessary?

7. Have I ever been a fair-weather friend to someone, and how can I change that behavior?
    - What situations or insecurities have caused me to be less than supportive, and what steps can I take to be a better friend?

8. What steps can I take to strengthen the bonds with my true friends?
    - What specific actions or conversations could enhance trust, communication, or shared experiences with those who matter most to me?

9. How do I protect myself from being hurt by those who only seek friendship out of self-interest?
    - What boundaries do I need to set or reinforce to safeguard my emotional well-being without closing myself off to new relationships?

10. What does it mean to me to be a true friend, and how can I embody those qualities more fully?
    - What can I consciously practice every day to better reflect the values of loyalty, honesty, and kindness in my friendships?

Chapter 13: The Challenge Of Life

The challenge of life is one of the most profound journeys we'll ever face. As we step into the future, the path before us is uncertain, filled with obstacles we must navigate. Each one presents an opportunity to learn and grow, but it also forces us out of our comfort zones. This is where life truly begins—where excitement and joy mingle with fear and anxiety, and where we discover what we're truly capable of. The challenge lies not just in overcoming these hurdles, but in finding the balance between embracing the unknown and staying grounded in our values and goals. Life's lessons come from both the victories and the stumbles, and the beauty of this challenge is that every step forward, whether it's smooth or difficult, shapes who we become.

Life doesn't hand out maps or compasses to guide us. Instead, we are tasked with forging our own way, often given opportunities but never guarantees. It's up to us to seize those moments, prove our worth, and strive to live our best lives. Along the way, we encounter successes, accolades, and moments of triumph, but we also face fear, pain, loss, and regret. These are not failures to dwell on, but lessons to revisit and learn from. Life's true challenge is not about avoiding difficulty but learning from it, growing stronger, and becoming a doer—a finisher—who takes control of their own story.

The challenge of life is never simple, but that's what makes it the most important one we'll ever undertake. Through failure and success, joy and sorrow, we discover that life isn't about the absence of difficulty but about the strength we gain through perseverance. It teaches us to lead ourselves, to step into the unknown with confidence, and to embrace every part of the journey—because it's in the struggle that we find our greatest victories and learn the essence of who we are meant to be.

A Tale Written In The Stars

"Amidst the twists of fate and the landscapes of our lives, a lone traveler presses on. With each step on this winding path—where shadows dance with light, and obstacles beckon strength—fear and excitement intertwine. It is here, in the journey itself, that we discover not just paths but possibilities, guided by the silent stirrings of our own brave hearts."

—Unknown

A Tale Written in the Stars

To transform one's stars
Is to call through to one's own heaven—
To forage the forsaken,
To leave behind one's past,
And see the future yet to come.

Spring calls—
A journey unset, gladly called forth,
A mystery in the unknowing,
A wanton captivation of the future.

Still, a hint of blackness is overpowering.
You understand not what choices must be made,
Solely relying on wisdom—
You complete that which most allow to fade.

No fate can call you forward,
No future is set to be unattained.
Willfully, you accept your role
And partake in the role played.

You are distracted by the question—
Less, you are not what you can be.
Through the eyes of the looking glass,
The image can be false and not sufficiently seen.

One can never see through one's own eyes
And sense the true image of what makes one who they will become.
Only through the actions of courage and honor
Will true life journey forward, exceeding in all things done.

My eyes fasten on the journey that leaves no trail—
No direction charted,
Only the ill-gotten illusion
And its bitter taste left to assail.

A Tale Written In The Stars
10 Questions to Reflect On,

1. What has been the most defining moment on your life journey so far, and how has it shaped the path you're on today?
    - How have your beliefs or personal values shifted as a result of this moment, and what lasting impact has it had on your decisions?
2. Reflecting on your life's path, what have been the biggest obstacles you've faced, and how have you overcome them?
    - What internal and external resources did you rely on to get through these challenges, and how have they changed you?
3. How do you maintain your direction and purpose when the path seems unclear or fraught with challenges?
    - What practices or mindsets help you refocus and regain clarity when you feel lost or uncertain?
4. Can you identify a time when a seemingly insurmountable challenge turned into a valuable lesson? What did you learn?
    - How did this lesson reshape your understanding of failure or adversity, and how do you apply it today?
5. How do you balance the fear and excitement that come with stepping into the unknown?
    - What strategies help you embrace uncertainty, and how do you stay grounded while moving forward?
6. In what ways have your experiences of success and failure contributed to your growth as an individual?
    - How do you measure growth—both in moments of victory and in times of difficulty?

7. How do you decide when to follow a well-trodden path and when to forge your own way?
    - What factors do you weigh when choosing between safety and risk, and how do you trust your instincts in those moments?
8. What strategies do you use to cope with the stormy patches of life and to appreciate the sunny ones?
    - How do you maintain resilience during tough times, and what practices help you savor the joyful moments?
9. Who or what has been your compass on this journey, helping you to find your way during times of uncertainty?
    - How do you connect with this guiding force, and what do you do when you feel disconnected or unsure of your direction?
10. Looking ahead, what steps can you take today to prepare for the next phase of your life's journey?
    - What intentions or goals can you set right now to ensure that you're ready to embrace future opportunities and challenges?

Chapter 14: Loss

Grief is one of the most profound and difficult experiences we face in life, especially when it involves losing someone who means the world to us—a father, mother, sister, or anyone close to our hearts. While we may know deep down that loss is inevitable, the reality of it is still shattering. Grief comes in many forms, not just in the loss of family, friends, or pets, but also in moments of great tragedy, like war or natural disasters that claim countless lives. The weight of grief can be overwhelming, leaving you feeling broken, disconnected, and emotionally unstable. One moment you may cry uncontrollably, and the next, you feel nothing at all, lost in a fog of numbness. It's an emotional rollercoaster that can make you feel like a shadow of your former self. Yet, how we deal with that grief is what defines the healing process—taking the pain and turning it into something constructive, something that honors the memory of the person or people we've lost.

Remembering them is one of the most powerful ways to commemorate their spirit. The wonderful times you shared, the moments of joy, laughter, and love, all become part of the legacy they leave behind. These memories are not just a way to remember; they are a way to keep their presence alive in your heart. Grief teaches us about connection—the deep bonds we form, and the aching void when those bonds are severed. It also teaches us about resilience. You must find the strength to confront the grief head-on, not to move on or forget, but to accept the loss and what it means for your life. Blame, anger, and spiritual doubt may arise, but these too are part of the process. Reaching out to close friends, or finding solace in community, can help ease the pain of separation, allowing you to slowly heal. Ultimately, finding meaning in the loss is crucial, not just in the act of separation but in the truth it holds about life's fragility and the importance of love and connection.

The Pain Remains

"Grief is not the final chapter, but a passage we all must walk through. It is in the letting go that we begin to heal, for the pain we carry is not meant to define us but to cleanse us. The love we shared with those we've lost never fades, and though their presence feels absent, their light remains—guiding us through the darkest moments. In accepting this, we find the strength to live again, knowing that every loss is a lesson in faith, resilience, and the enduring power of connection." —Unknown

The Pain Remains

Our tears are never-ending,
Our cries are overrun.
Situations of mass determination
Are shattered, completely undone.

The hopelessness is maddening
When loss comes without aim.
The circle of infinite possibilities
Requires suffering to feel pain.

Can one let go of that which is so tightly grasped?
Can we see that the loss we feel is not the end?
Can I understand this pain is required for cleansing?
Can I ever let go and believe again?

When one is lost to a second of hazard,
When one is lost to an intrepid moment,
When one is lost to an instance of frailty,
When one is lost to sudden idiocy,
The pain remains.

The grieving is recurring,
Like a wound that never heals.
Mourning only delays the trip,
Leaving an emptiness strikingly real.

No matter how strongly we feel,
No matter how we let emotion control,

Emotional shadows can be just as deceiving
When we turn from the truth we consciously know.

You are restless, feeling alone,
Knowing they are no longer there
To share in your trials and triumphs,
Holding on because you care.

How life can be ripped away
As unprepared as you might be,
There is no end to infinite creation
That only in death can be revealed.

I have let go of what I tightly grasped.
I can see the loss I feel is not the end.
I understand this pain is required for cleansing.
I have let go and held on again.

When one is lost to accidental deception,
When one is lost to lack of faith,
When one is lost to aimless desire,
When one is lost to mortality's face,
The pain remains.

Their earthly journey has ended,
For mortal time is short to pass.
Their memory is never concluded,
And their spirit will infinitely last.

Why do we hold on to this pain,
To torture that which is already done?
Understand its reasons,

Allowing you both to be one.

We create a rational illustration
Of the joyous times we shared.
Memories are always lasting,
But we must be unafraid to be aware.

Where do fallen spirits go
When death comes calling?
We feel its cold uncertainty,
Powerful and enthralling.

Visions of emptiness are emerging,
Shadows, visions for you to see.
In all actuality, it comes down to decision—
Letting go is all the freedom we need.

They are with us even now,
Sharing breath, words, and thoughts.
Playing an active role in our lives,
Mirroring images time has forgot.

Life and death are transposed,
For life and death go hand in hand.
Energy changing form
Is the cycle of God's plan.

Freedom of the soul comes from letting go—
Letting go of the pain,
Letting go of the regret,
Letting go like light breaking through the dark,
Letting go to reclaim the heart.

We must not be selfish, for the journey requires faith—
Faith in ourselves,
Faith in our hearts,
Faith in our Maker,
That all will be done.

The pain is dealt with slowly,
We shouldn't forget, and stay aware,
That in focusing its direction constructively,
We realize they will always be there to share.

A loss is always personal,
Unique to all involved each time.
Visit each new day with wonder,
And inner peace is all you will find.

I have let go of what I tightly grasped.
I can see that the loss I feel is not the end.
I understand this pain is required for cleansing.
I have let go, and started living again.

Our lives are filled with hope,
Our hearts are shattered and torn.
Though the pain remains,
Their light shines evermore.

The Pain Remains

10 Questions to Reflect On,

1. How has the loss I've experienced changed my perception of life and its fragility?
    - Reflect on how this loss has altered your worldview or your understanding of life's impermanence.
2. What emotions am I holding back in my grieving process, and why?
    - Explore whether you are suppressing feelings like anger, sadness, or guilt and how that affects your healing.
3. How do I honor the memory of the person I've lost while continuing to move forward?
    - Consider how you can keep their memory alive without being trapped by the weight of grief.
4. What does this loss teach me about love and connection?
    - Reflect on the relationship you had and what insights or lessons about love, vulnerability, and connection it provides.
5. What am I afraid to confront in my grief, and how is that fear impacting my healing?
    - Explore any fears or avoidance you may feel around truly processing your emotions.
6. How has this loss affected my faith or spiritual beliefs?
    - Think about whether the experience of loss has strengthened, weakened, or transformed your spiritual perspective.
7. How do I cope with feelings of guilt or regret about the person I lost?

- Reflect on unresolved emotions or unfinished conversations and how they influence your grieving.

8. What support do I need in my grieving journey, and how can I ask for it?
    - Identify the kind of help you need—whether from others, therapy, or spiritual practices—and how to reach out for it.

9. How do I find meaning or purpose in life after loss?
    - Consider how the experience of loss might lead you to discover new purpose, insights, or changes in direction.

10. What steps can I take to slowly let go of the pain while keeping the love?
    - Reflect on how you can allow healing to occur without feeling that it diminishes the love or connection you shared with the person.

Chapter 15: Unmasked

Life is a stage, and we are all performers, taking on the roles of actor, director, producer, and audience in the grand show of existence. We wear different costumes, don masks, and play countless roles for a variety of reasons. At work, we perform for our managers, colleagues, and customers, carefully curating our actions and words to fit the expectations of the setting. In social situations— whether purchasing something, meeting new people, or even dating—we slip into other roles, portraying versions of ourselves that may not be entirely genuine. It's often easier to follow a script that society has written for us, rather than to write our own lines and live authentically. But as we take on these roles, we must ask ourselves: are we being true to who we are, or are we performing for the benefit of others, living a life shaped by their expectations?

From childhood, we instinctively knew how to play make-believe. We imagined ourselves as soldiers, adventurers, firefighters, or royalty—yet, in the midst of that fantasy, we were still our genuine selves. Children have the remarkable ability to engage in these roles while remaining authentic, unburdened by the opinions of others. But as we grow older, society molds us, teaching us that the approval of others holds more weight than being true to ourselves. The roles we play as adults are often less about joy and more about survival—adopting personas to fit in, to avoid judgment, or to gain acceptance. Over time, these roles can confine us, preventing us from moving forward and living our most authentic life. The key to breaking free is self-validation. It's okay to enjoy moments of make-believe, but we must also step off the stage, leave the actor in the dressing room, and embrace the person we truly are. Only then can we live fully and without the weight of others' expectations, staying true to the genuine self we were meant to be.

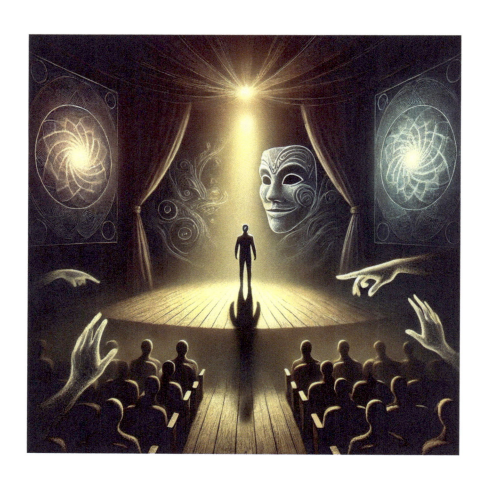

The Show

"Life is a stage where we often play roles crafted by expectations and fears, hiding behind masks to shield ourselves from the truths we don't wish to confront. We perform not for others, but to deceive ourselves, living within the comfort of a script that keeps us complacent. Only by stepping beyond the shadows and breaking free from the roles imposed on us can we truly discover who we are and reclaim our authentic selves."

—Unknown

The Show

Take a glimpse into the future—
As you see it, is it clear?
Did you deceive yourself into a false understanding,
Or is it something complete by design?
You, the designer,
Not taking part in your own project.

Captivate your audience,
When the only audience is you—
The actor you are,
Standing alone on a stage of shadows,
Envisioning yourself clearly for all to see,
Offering change because you have no control.

Why are you idle?
You choose to be alone,
To yourself, so clear, so cold.
The show you put on
Offers no comfort, no warmth—
Only the dissatisfaction that controls.

Excise your fear.
The life you have now
Is not the life you must live.
What example do you need?
What proof do you require
When the truth is fractured by your freedom—

Relying on others' opinions
To shape your design?

Jump from your shell of complacency,
And soar into your own role.
Your will can be so complete
In making decisions,
Yet you share them with others,
Forsaking your own for their views.

You can be justified in your outlook—
But make sure your outlook
Isn't clouded by foolish pride.
Pride can be an incredible distraction,
And the real self remains alone,
Deliberately denied.

A journey in life requires taking a chance.
The fight for this is a true necessity,
Where the real self is left alone,
Atoning for decisions
We've learned to rely on.

What more do you need to learn?
What role, what script is required
To finally understand,
To finally know
That the face you wear in life
Is the mask of the false person,
Acting in the show.

The Show
10 Questions to Reflect On,

1. What roles am I playing in my life, and are they authentic to who I really am?

    ◦ Reflect on the roles you perform in various aspects of life (personal, professional, social) and whether they align with your true self.

2. In what areas of my life do I feel like I am merely acting rather than truly living?

    ◦ Consider where you feel you're going through the motions instead of being fully present and genuine.

3. What mask am I wearing, and why am I afraid to remove it?

    ◦ Explore the persona you present to the world and what fears keep you from revealing your true self.

4. How have I allowed external opinions to shape my decisions and identity?

    ◦ Reflect on how much influence others have on your choices and sense of self, and whether this has led you away from your authentic path.

5. What stage in my life feels most controlled by shadows or fear, and how can I bring light to it?

    ◦ Identify areas where fear or uncertainty dominate and think about how to reclaim control or shift perspective.

6. What truth am I avoiding, and how is that affecting my ability to move forward?

- Consider any difficult realities or truths you've been reluctant to face and the impact this avoidance has on your growth.

7. Am I designing my life, or am I letting it be designed for me?
    - Reflect on whether you are consciously shaping your path or if you are passively allowing circumstances or others to direct your life.

8. How does pride influence my decisions, and is it holding me back from being authentic?
    - Explore the role of pride in your choices and whether it's helping or hindering your journey to self-discovery and authenticity.

9. What proof or validation am I constantly seeking from others, and how can I shift this need inward?
    - Think about where you rely on external approval and how you might begin to find self-acceptance and validation from within.

10. What would my life look like if I broke free from the scripts I've been following?
    - Imagine what changes would occur if you let go of societal expectations, old patterns, or false personas, and fully embraced your authentic self.

Chapter 16: Temptation vs. Inner Strength

We live our lives navigating a path we set for ourselves, often without a clear map, but with the hope that it is paved with honor and respect for both ourselves and others. Along this journey, we encounter numerous temptations—distractions that can overwhelm us and pull us away from our true purpose. Living in search of fleeting pleasures, whether material or physical, can lead us down a destructive path, leaving us feeling powerless and tormented by our own weaknesses. These temptations create chains that bind us, controlling our decisions and shaping our lives in ways that may not align with who we truly are. The path we walk should be one we work for, a road built with intention and care, but sometimes, the illusion of hunger for more clouds our vision, leading us astray. The pursuit of power or satisfaction can hold us captive, guiding us to make choices that do not reflect our true desires.

It is important to remember that we have free will—the ability to choose our own direction and to prioritize inner substance over external gains. In today's society, social media bombards us daily with expectations about how we should look, act, eat, and live. While social media itself isn't inherently harmful, it can sway us, pushing us further from our true nature if we aren't careful. The key is to remove pride and control the ego, to ask ourselves if the torment we feel is caused by temptations or needs that do not align with our inherent nature. If the choices we make are not true to who we are, we know we've strayed from our path. But the more we work at understanding ourselves and resisting these temptations, the more we will realize when we are on the right path—one rooted in authenticity, purpose, and meaning.

Torment

"Within the quiet darkness of the soul, there lies a battle—one not of sword or shield, but of will. The torment that grows inside us is like a whisper in the wind, feeding on our weaknesses, tempting us with fleeting pleasures while binding us in chains of our own making. We walk a path, unsure if it's chosen or forced upon us, where control is an illusion and the torment patiently waits, feeding on fear, doubt, and desire. Only through facing the shadows of this internal conflict can we begin to free ourselves from the hold of our own torment, though it may reside within us, waiting, until we find our truth." —Unknown

Torment

The night sky is dark,
The wind is stagnant,
Offering a hint of chill.
An ominous voice calls out to me,
Fighting to break my will.

There is a hunger growing inside me,
Like a starving little child.
It entices me with earthly pleasures,
A festering eruption that lets my soul grow wild.

I remember when I was young,
I could feel the change within—
Growing past my failures,
My dual destiny was set to begin.

I can tell you when I felt this torment—
It was like a sharp blade unsheathed,
Buried deep inside my soul,
Forcefully received.

I felt the mortal conflict,
That offered as much as it would demand.
Wanting it to take control of me,
Yet in my acceptance,
I realized it was never planned.

Sometimes I feel I've chosen this path,
For the way it makes me feel—
Inviting its power on occasion,
Like a handshake that seals the deal.

Its purpose is to infuse its power,
To take complete control,
Concentrating on my weakness,
Until I crave it to show me more.

You see, we all possess this weakness.
This torment is necessary to understand.
But tolerating it,
Letting it fester inside,
Will fulfill its concealed plan.

Listen for silent sounds of power
That can corrupt your dreams and soul—
Placing thoughts, twisting reason,
Until you lose all control.

The time to believe is now,
For the end of free will might be on the rise.
Its powerful influence builds,
As our weak souls demise.

One day I will know in my heart
If this path is truly right for me.
But until that day of judgment comes,
The torment will impatiently reside in me.

Torment

10 Questions to Reflect On,

1. What internal battles am I facing, and how do they manifest in my daily life?
   - Reflect on the struggles that weigh on you and how they affect your thoughts, actions, and decisions.
2. How does the temptation of earthly pleasures influence my sense of control?
   - Consider how external temptations or desires may pull you away from what you truly value or desire for yourself.
3. In what ways have I felt powerless or controlled by forces outside my will?
   - Explore moments in your life where you've felt that you've lost control, either to circumstances or internal conflict.
4. What part of me is drawn to the very thing that torments me?
   - Reflect on why certain challenges or temptations seem alluring even though they bring pain or conflict.
5. How do I distinguish between what I've chosen and what has been imposed on me?
   - Consider whether you are actively choosing your path, or if you feel certain forces are guiding you without your consent.
6. What fears or weaknesses am I allowing to control my decisions?
   - Explore the fears or vulnerabilities that might be giving rise to internal conflict or torment.
7. What power am I handing over to others or to external forces?

- Reflect on how much of your autonomy and control you are giving away to others' opinions, societal expectations, or fleeting desires.

8. How do I balance accepting my weaknesses with the desire to overcome them?
    - Consider how you can acknowledge your flaws without allowing them to control you.

9. What role does pride or ego play in my inner conflict?
    - Reflect on whether pride or ego is making it harder for you to confront or resolve your torment.

10. When the time comes to make a final judgment on my path, how will I know if it was right for me?
    - Think about how you will measure whether your choices, struggles, and internal battles ultimately aligned with your true self.

Chapter 17: Breaking The Cycle

Life often feels like a trap. Each day, we wake up, go through the motions—eating breakfast, cleaning up, getting the family ready, and heading off to work. The hours drag on as we wait for a break, longing for a few moments to ourselves. Then we return home, only to realize the tasks we couldn't get to during the week are now waiting for the weekend. The cycle is endless, with little time for genuine rest or reflection. We chase these moments of respite, but they are fleeting, drowned out by the demands of daily life. We become cogs in a machine, consumed by the need to keep up with the bills, the responsibilities, and the expectations placed on us. House payments, car payments, medical bills, student loans, and credit card debt pile up, and we are constantly told to buy more, spend more, keeping us in a state of perpetual consumption.

As we get caught up in the illusions of success and security, it becomes harder to see the truth behind all that desire. From childhood, we are trained to seek stability, to follow a path that is supposed to bring comfort and safety. But this path often leaves us caged, stuck in a system that values complacency over freedom. The stability we think we are working toward is not true freedom—it's a form of control, a carefully constructed illusion that keeps us from challenging the status quo. We settle into the grind, accepting that this is just the way life is, without questioning whether it's really the life we want to live. In doing so, we avoid the challenge of creating something more meaningful for ourselves.

While we all have to work and provide, it's essential to become more aware of the "mill" we are grinding for. Are we working toward a life of freedom that we'll only experience when we're too old to enjoy it? Or are we reconciling ourselves to a life of toil because we've been conditioned to accept it as inevitable? The key is to live authentically, to survive and thrive by producing something truly great—something that goes beyond the consumer-driven cycle we've been taught to follow. By breaking free from the traps of consumption, we can begin to shape a life of purpose and fulfillment, one where we are not just surviving but genuinely living.

The Mill

"We are cogs in a machine, spinning through illusions of choice and truth, unaware of the patterns that mold us. In the vastness of existence, we are both the creators and the captives of our own design—performing in a world where the sky holds no answers, only reflections of the lies we've embraced." —Unknown

The Mill

The sky opens wide, a vast façade,
Shadows hidden in shades of light, dressed in elaborate disguise.
Futures unfold for those who trust its essence,
Steady for those who exaggerate its lie.

A swirling vortex engulfs your awareness,
Drawing you into a virtual experiment.
Surrounded, consumed by a classified assimilation,
Simply answering,
"I exist."

We glance past the intricate symbols of life,
Refusing to wake from our sweet, sour dream.
We walk alone in simulations,
Crying out from a nameless source,
Learning nothing, teaching the invisible.

The sky knows no boundaries;
It simply is.
It holds you together,
And lets creation begin.

It sharpens your tendencies,
So you can grasp your deepest desires—
But molds you in a pattern,
Empty and alone.

Where is truth?
Is it lost in this whimsical carnival,
Where we are caged, staged, trained to perform?
Offered up as examples without excitement,
Portrayed as fools beneath the lights.

The Mill

10 Questions to Reflect On,

1. In what ways do I feel trapped or controlled by forces outside of my own will?
   - Reflect on whether there are societal, cultural, or internal pressures that confine you to a role you didn't choose.
2. Am I living authentically, or am I performing a version of myself that others expect to see?
   - Consider how much of your life is a genuine expression of who you are versus what you think others want you to be.
3. What illusions am I holding onto that prevent me from seeing the truth about my life?
   - Reflect on any beliefs or perceptions you have that may be distorting reality or keeping you from understanding yourself fully.
4. How do I reconcile the difference between what I desire and what I feel I must accept?
   - Examine the conflict between your true desires and the compromises you've made in life.
5. What "patterns" am I stuck in, and how do they shape my sense of purpose?
   - Identify recurring habits or ways of thinking that keep you in the same cycles, and consider how they affect your sense of self and purpose.

6. Where do I seek meaning, and is it coming from within or from external validation?
    - Reflect on whether your search for meaning is driven by your inner values or by the need for approval and recognition from others.
7. How do I balance my need for stability with my longing for freedom?
    - Explore the tension between security and the desire to break free from routines or societal expectations.
8. Am I aware of the ways in which I might be "caged, staged, and trained" by life's circumstances?
    - Consider how much of your identity has been shaped by external forces and how that influences your actions and decisions.
9. What truths am I avoiding because they challenge the life I've built?
    - Reflect on whether there are uncomfortable truths you may be suppressing to maintain your current way of life.
10. If I were to break free from these illusions, what would my life look like?
    - Imagine a life where you are no longer bound by societal expectations, external pressures, or false beliefs. How would you live differently?

Chapter 18: Embracing The Journey

Life is truly an adventure, an unfolding journey that starts in childhood and stretches into old age, constantly pulling us toward the search for meaning. It is filled with wonder and excitement, but also with moments of uncertainty. As we travel through life, we face pain, doubt, and fear that can overwhelm us, leading to moments where it feels as though we are spiraling downward. Yet, this adventure is part of our human experience—full of both happiness and suffering, growth and setbacks. We must continue to strive, to push forward and upward despite the challenges, knowing that each step, whether joyous or painful, adds to the depth of our journey.

The search for meaning doesn't always yield clear answers, but there is tremendous value in the pursuit itself. Along the way, we dream, we fight, and we pray for each new opportunity to advance, creating and sharing our aspirations. Yet, in the midst of this, we often wear masks and build walls, shaping ourselves to fit others' expectations rather than embracing our true selves. Our memories— like a scrapbook—can either fill our consciousness with purpose or dull it with regret. To live this adventure authentically, we must recognize what we are searching for and reinforce our true identity at every turn, confronting each challenge directly instead of hiding behind personas that are not our own.

Ultimately, the purpose of this journey is to find meaning, even when life feels overwhelming. We are in control of our path, even when it doesn't seem that way. It takes faith in ourselves and in our intentions to face struggles head-on, as we were always meant to do. By letting go of the personas that mask our true selves, we stop delaying our progress. Instead, we honor the human adventure we are meant to travel, embracing each twist and turn as a necessary part of discovering who we truly are.

The Human Adventure

"The human adventure is a journey of constant searching—searching for meaning, identity, and purpose in a world that often feels overwhelming. We hold onto memories, dreams, and faith, only to find ourselves lost at times, questioning everything we once believed in. But in the stillness of our struggles, we learn that the pain, doubt, and fear are not the end—they are part of the process. This adventure is not about finding all the answers but about embracing the uncertainty, knowing that growth comes from both the joy and the suffering. In the end, it's the act of continuing to reach, to try, and to dream, that defines our journey and keeps us moving forward." —Unknown

The Human Adventure

The human adventure has just started.
All the feelings,
The imagination,
The happiness,
The sadness—
This mystery of enchantment offers only conclusions.

Returning to old ways brings constancy.
My mind envisions nothing that makes sense.
Closing the door, I forget all the things that matter.
Then again, what really does matter?

Losing all that is offered to one
Can only be seen as an outsider.
Seeing it within, we no longer have control—
Only a false sense of what we are really trying to accomplish.

Holding onto mementos and dreams,
We use them,
Empower them to control,
Control the things we no longer believe in.

My hands are shaking.
My heart is still.
There is no longer any movement,
Only stillness, frozen.

I cannot believe anymore.
The faith I once held onto so tightly
Has found a way to escape.
Alone once again, I am lost.

Putting it all on the line,
Committed to life's aim,
I run away from what matters.
Whispering voices speak—
I no longer care.

What is it that I see
In the middle of everything?
I am blind,
Troubled,
Reaching out,
Returning empty-handed.

I have no answers.
I no longer know or value what I search for.
I keep trying,
Praying for a chance
To find my independence and importance again.

I dream of sharing my dreams,
Misunderstanding that it's only a dream.
By daylight, returning to life's reason,
Once again, I wear the mask.

The walls of my mind are covered with pictures of my history—
A slideshow of friends, family, happiness, sadness, and regret.
Dull in my consideration, contained in my search,

With a wandering mind,
Placating me,
Being all to everyone, except myself.

As close as I come so many times,
Racing to the finish,
Not realizing the truth—
Always finishing alone.

Take me away.
Let me take a chance.
Always waiting,
The patient one,
As everything passes me by.

Will I ever get it right?
Will I ever fight for my truth?
Continuing to dwell in my own personal reality,
Leaving before I ever decide to stay.

I am that child who is afraid of the dark,
Hiding underneath my bed,
Crying,
Begging for it all to end,
Running away.

Worthless talent—
Sweetest pleasure from defeat.
Alive within the motions,
Coming to the moment,
Breaking in two.

I gain strength from this pain,
Offering it to others to learn and understand—
That you are not alone.

There is a tourniquet binding me,
Constricting me.
Rain clouds hover high above.
No one ever told me this was how it would be.
Finding this, surprised and afraid,
I fold.

Can I ever forget and let go of what I have been taught—
The things that I have learned?
I honestly believe I can't forget.
I need to live through to the end—
The end of the human adventure,
An adventure that will last forever.

The Human Adventure
10 Questions to Reflect On,

1. What am I truly searching for in life, and how has this quest shaped my journey so far?
   - Reflect on your inner desires, goals, and whether you feel you are on the path to achieving them or still searching.
2. How do I define my identity, and has that definition evolved as I've faced challenges?
   - Consider whether your sense of self has shifted as you've encountered life's struggles and how that has impacted you.
3. What is my purpose in life, and am I actively pursuing it or waiting for it to reveal itself?
   - Reflect on whether you feel driven by a clear purpose or if you're still seeking one, and how this affects your actions.
4. Why do I often feel overwhelmed by the demands of life, and how can I manage this feeling better?
   - Explore the sources of stress or pressure in your life and whether you can shift your perspective to handle them more effectively.
5. In what ways do my memories influence my present, and am I holding onto them too tightly or too loosely?
   - Consider the role of past experiences, whether they empower or limit you, and how they shape your current worldview.
6. Do my dreams reflect my true desires, or are they illusions created by external influences?

- Reflect on whether the aspirations you pursue are genuinely yours or shaped by societal, familial, or external expectations.

7. What role does faith play in my life, and how has it changed as I've faced personal struggles?

    - Explore your relationship with faith, spirituality, or belief systems and how they guide or challenge you in times of difficulty.

8. How do I balance the tension between holding on to the past and moving forward into the future?

    - Reflect on how past experiences, memories, or regrets weigh on you and whether they are preventing you from growing.

9. Am I wearing a "mask" to please others, and how does this affect my sense of fulfillment and truth?

    - Think about whether you are living authentically or if you feel compelled to meet the expectations of others, and how this impacts your personal satisfaction.

10. What does "success" look like for me in this human adventure, and does it align with what truly matters?

    - Consider how you define success—whether it's career, relationships, personal growth, or something else—and whether your definition aligns with your core values.

Chapter 19: Strength In Hope

Hope is defined as a feeling of expectation and desire for a particular outcome or event, often tied to optimism and belief that things will improve or turn out positively. It's an integral part of our human experience, pushing us to continue striving toward our goals even when the path is unclear. We understand that adversity and uncertainty are inevitable, but hope provides the possibility for better circumstances, allowing us to believe that what we seek is within reach. It is that quiet motivator, driving us to achieve something meaningful despite the obstacles in our way. The phrase "I hope for something" or "I hope this turns out the way I planned" reflects how hope influences our decisions. Sometimes it works out in our favor, and other times we are deceived by false expectations. Still, hope remains a fundamental part of our journey, a light that we follow in our pursuit of purpose.

But what happens when we lose hope? When we find ourselves at the end of the rope, only to realize it wasn't long enough to reach the bottom, it can feel like the world is closing in. Do we allow this defeat to consume us, curling up in despair and surrendering to the weight of disappointment? While it's natural to feel disheartened in those moments, we must resist the temptation to wallow. Instead, we need to manifest truths in our lives, reflect on our past for guidance, and remember that losing hope in one moment doesn't mean we are lost forever. The key is not to hide behind a mask of false confidence when hope fails, but rather to reaffirm our foundation—who we are and what we truly want to achieve. Hope, after all, is not a guarantee of success, but it is the spark that can bring us out of darkness and propel us toward the light of possibility.

Hope alone is not enough—it must be reinforced by action, commitment, and dedication. To truly harness the power of hope, we must back it up with hard work and perseverance. You can't simply begin a project, put in minimal effort, and expect hope to carry it to success. It requires heart, soul, and consistency at every turn. As I've mentioned many times before, we all have to work hard in this life, not just hope for the best, but put in the effort to make it happen. When we do this, hope is validated, strengthened by the knowledge that we have done everything possible to achieve our goals. In the end, hope becomes more than just a wish—it becomes a driving force that helps us create a life worth hoping for.

Hope Has Brought You Out

"Hope is both a light and a deception, a force that pulls us toward clarity yet often leads us deeper into the maze of self-doubt and questioning. In the search for meaning, we grapple with love, loss, and the uncertainty of our own identity. This poem reflects the internal battle between wanting to understand ourselves and fearing the truth we may find. It reminds us that, in the end, we are strangers to our own reflection, struggling to reconcile our hopes with the reality we often run from." —Unknown

Hope Has Brought You Out

Hope has stirred a mystery within me,
Engaging me, yet far from fault.
Meant to be full of hope, but harmony is lost
At the heart of Heaven's gate.
Blindness hides within love and the loss of self—
Allowed to exist, but never fully grasped.

Such deception is inevitable, for within harmony
There is no freedom from sacrifice.
No apathy for the one who longs.
Can the laughter of the careless man be heard,
Resolved, in a moment unseen but deeply absorbed?

Feelings change, bringing understanding—
But do we truly hear the call?
Do we allow ourselves to listen,
Choosing what we know,
And what we only think we understand?

There is anger, there is rage,
And unto the giver, there is no rival.
Deception, removal, the loss of clarity,
Reserved for the unwilling one.
The device is the motive, the instance a reminder—
Running toward a passage, secret to the blind.

Blindness recalls the sickness within,
A longing that grows louder in its silence.
The eyes are the path to losing oneself,
While death and arrogance whisper their truth.

Why?
For knowledge grows where we must feed patience,
Remembering what and who we need.

As memories pass, they offer instinct—
No matter how long they last,
Memories fade,
And our own reality dies with them.

What am I, really?
Mistakes keep screaming out,
Calling me back.
How long will deception soothe the pain of these reminders?
We are strangers, frozen within ourselves,
The child left alone without knowing why.

Looking in the mirror, I see a reflection—
But do I truly see what's there?
Am I afraid of punishment,
Or unwilling to be everyone?
Then again, am I really anyone at all?

The masquerade calls out,
Its madness to blame.
It forces its will upon the willing,
Offering a false truce.
But there is no peace.

There is no relief—
Only the endless journey of a hopeless man,
Reckoning with life, waiting for it to fulfill itself.

Hope Has Brought You Out
10 Questions to Reflect On,

1. What does hope mean to me, and how does it influence my decisions?
   - Reflect on how hope drives your actions or affects your mindset, and whether it serves as a guiding force or a source of confusion.
2. In what ways have I deceived myself while trying to hold on to hope?
   - Consider whether you have held onto illusions or false beliefs in your pursuit of hope, and how that has impacted your journey.
3. What am I truly seeking through hope—peace, purpose, or something else?
   - Reflect on what you hope to gain from your search, and whether it aligns with your deeper needs or desires.
4. How do I respond when I lose faith or when hope seems distant?
   - Explore how you handle moments of doubt or despair and whether they lead you to grow or pull you further away from understanding.
5. Am I afraid of fully seeing myself, or am I afraid of what I might discover?
   - Reflect on whether fear of self-discovery is holding you back from truly understanding who you are and how you navigate life's challenges.
6. How does the concept of 'blindness' manifest in my life—what truths am I avoiding?

- Consider whether you are ignoring certain realities about yourself, your relationships, or your circumstances, and how that impacts your growth.

7. What role do memories, both painful and joyful, play in shaping my current sense of self?
    - Reflect on how your past, including both its highs and lows, has influenced your identity and the way you view yourself today.

8. How do I balance the need for hope with the reality of struggle and suffering?
    - Explore whether you are able to hold onto hope while accepting life's challenges, or if the pursuit of hope sometimes leads you away from acknowledging hard truths.

9. Am I wearing a "mask" to hide my true self from others, and why?
    - Reflect on whether you feel the need to present a certain version of yourself to the world, and how this impacts your ability to be authentic.

10. What steps can I take to reconcile who I think I am with who I truly am?
    - Consider how you can begin to integrate the different aspects of your identity, confronting fears, accepting imperfections, and embracing your true self.

Chapter 20: United In Purpose, Divided by Perception

The past is a powerful teacher, yet we often fail to learn its lessons. It's a reflection of both our successes and our deepest mistakes, a reminder of what we have done—right and wrong. Time has the power to forge change, but that process often comes with pain, no matter how we try to avoid it. Today, the world offers more freedom and opportunity than at any other point in history, yet we find ourselves more divided than ever. This division is not just about policy or personal differences—it's rooted in how we see one another, how we choose to separate rather than unite. Race, religion, and rights have become the defining points of our struggles, creating rifts in society that reflect a deeper, unresolved pain.

One of the greatest tragedies we face is that empathy, the ability to understand and share the feelings of others, has been lost in the noise. Instead of seeing the burdens that people of all races, backgrounds, and cultures carry, we brand each other with labels—quick to judge, slow to understand. Poverty, homelessness, violence, and hatred exist in every group, yet we focus on these differences as though they define us. We have become too consumed by anger, too eager to fuel that fire with the embers of the past. Instead of learning from history, we cling to it, using it as an excuse to spread hatred and division, forgetting that everyone, in some way, is broken. In doing so, we forsake the beauty of our diversity—the extraordinary richness of cultures and people that make this world what it is.

We've stopped celebrating the things that unite us, opting instead to nurture the divisions that tear us apart. Hatred and anger have overshadowed compassion and cooperation. People close their hearts, holding onto mistakes that have already been addressed, allowing grudges and anger to shape their actions. But if we are to build a future that rises above the mistakes of the past, we must let go of these preconceived notions and learn to live together as one. We all share this planet, and regardless of race, nationality, or creed, we all suffer the consequences of division. The foundation we should be striving for is unity— recognizing that no one label can contain the complexities of an individual's character, and that our differences should be celebrated, not condemned.

When you hear voices spewing hatred, take a step back and ask yourself why. What is the root cause of this anger? Most people simply want to live in peace, to deal with their own problems without adding to the chaos. Will you allow yourself to be swept up in the current of hate, or will you search for solutions to heal the wounds of racism and division? Instead of relying on hatred as an easy answer, take the time to look deep within yourself and realize that we are all bound by the same destiny. One day, we will all face the end of our journey. The question is: will we spend that time in hatred, or will we work together to make this world a better place? The choice is ours.

Why

"In the fires of our past, we can either burn or be forged. The pain and mistakes we inherit must not be ignored, but faced with courage and understanding. Only through unbinding our minds and opening our hearts can we heal the divides that tear us apart. Unity, love, and truth are the only paths to a future where we can truly be free." —Unknown

Why

Why can't we live together in a world where brotherhood can be?
With visions of the future, seen through the eyes of those who truly see.
Are our hearts so cold that we cannot allow the freedom of self to thrive,
As we hold such a tight reign on ourselves,
Running in circles of confusion, struggling to survive?

Is the color of skin or the ideals of others a prerequisite for hatred?
Is the value of a culture so sacred that it cannot be understood by others?
Is the heart that lies deep inside us all encased in a tomb?
God created us in His image—a metaphor of hearts,
For we all come from our mother's womb.

Hatred is the question that lies deep at the heart of it all,
Where we show our ability to care, only when we feel our protected heart won't fall.
When our children begin to cry, do we stop and take a second look
Running to their side, stopping their pain, mending their hearts with the love we took?

Why is it that some can never lend and bend with the natural flow,
Inherent to us all, like the rising sun's glow?
Is our freedom so private that we've learned to fear our neighbor,
Exchanging liberty for fear, taking on this heavy labor?

I see a man, his heart grown cold,
Born without caring, feeling deeply alone.
He finds his comfort in the anger within his soul,

Sharpening his hatred until he loses grasp
A trade-off for control.

I see another man, his heart filled with love,
Born with warmth from others, touched by God above. He finds comfort
in caring, as his values and morals grow,
Sharpening his skills of giving, never tiring, keeping a steady flow.

These two men are the same,
Born of different times,
But reality has changed them both,
And they're left alone, fighting for a place denied.

The ring of courage is forsaken,
When life's example is filled with fraud and ill-taken.
Fraudulent thoughts are not foreshadowed,
When the whispers of fools are heard and empowered.

Brutal blame is forced with a sharp, misshapen hand,
Filtered through voices, as blood drips on the land.
With thoughts twisted, and the road winding ahead,
Searing anger clouds the way, carrying a heavy dread.

Warped by time, reality bends,
Anguish screamed aloud without end.
Fear stands as our true banner,
With hollow words spoken, all meaning scattered.

The wind has spoken, but what does it say
About a history forgotten or twisted away?
Of all the beauty that time once knew,
Ignored with a breath—it was once the heart of you.

You look at your life, trying to focus somehow,
Fighting imagination that fades away now.
The wind still calls to those who seek the truth,
But only you can decide what you'll choose to do.

The past is filled with glory, not just myth
Hatred burns fires deep in the abyss.
Follow the passage deep within your past,
For without it, no future can ever last.

You must learn from past mistakes
And see the lighted way.
If the past is our roadmap,
Why don't we hold on and stay empowered each day?

We've become too closed to see what's real,
Like blinders on a horse, believing only what we feel.
Loss of illusion, loss of mystery, loss of imagination, loss of history
We can't let this loss close our narrow minds.
Without trust in ourselves, how can our faith not be blind?

There is good and bad in us all,
But we must begin to clearly see,
Past the veil of ignorance
Look through God's eyes to be free.

Can it be true, that we've all lost our way,
Forgetting the past and the mistakes that we made?
Don't we realize that all things return to show us the fire?
But maybe that pain is something we most desire.

Still, the fire can forge us, burn away the fear,
For the lessons we avoid will always reappear.
Only when we face the truth within,
Can we begin to resolve, and let healing begin.

Let us open our hearts, let us unbind our minds
To learn from the past, to heal the divide.
For in the ashes of yesterday's pain,
We will find the courage to rise again.

The future is not lost, not beyond repair,
If we can choose to see, to act, to care.
The light is waiting, just beyond our reach
But only unity, love, and truth can teach.

Why

10 Questions to Reflect On,

1. What barriers prevent me from fully understanding and empathizing with others, and how can I overcome them?
    - Reflect on whether internal biases or fears keep you from seeing others clearly and how you might break through these limitations.
2. How do I contribute to division in my relationships, community, or society, knowingly or unknowingly?
    - Consider whether your actions, words, or thoughts create distance or tension between yourself and others.
3. What role does fear play in how I view or interact with people who are different from me?
    - Reflect on how fear of the unknown or unfamiliar influences your behavior toward others, and whether it prevents connection.
4. In what ways do I allow past pain or anger to shape my worldview, and how can I move beyond that?
    - Explore whether past experiences of hurt or disappointment are still affecting how you see the world and others.
5. How have I benefited from cultural or social divisions, and how can I use that awareness to promote healing?
    - Reflect on any privileges or biases you've gained from these divisions and how you can shift that perspective to support unity.
6. Am I willing to open my heart and mind to perspectives that challenge my own beliefs?

- Consider whether you are truly open to hearing, understanding, and learning from people with different viewpoints.

7. What does unity mean to me, and what actions am I taking to cultivate it in my life?
    - Reflect on your personal definition of unity and whether you are actively fostering it in your interactions with others.

8. How can I learn from the mistakes of my past, or humanity's past, and apply those lessons to create a better future?
    - Explore how historical and personal mistakes can serve as lessons for positive change in your actions and outlook.

9. What steps can I take to let go of preconceived notions and judgments I hold about others?
    - Reflect on the ways you may prejudge people and how you can begin to release those judgments to foster better relationships.

10. How can I contribute to a world where love, truth, and understanding are the foundations of human interaction?
    - Think about what role you can play—no matter how small—in promoting love, truth, and unity in your community and beyond.

Chapter 21: Consumptions Downfall

On this planet, we share the Earth with an abundance of species—hundreds of thousands of creatures, big and small, gentle and fierce, all thriving on this blue, spinning marble in our solar system. From the very beginning, every species has fought for survival, each adapting to the environment to ensure its continued existence. Humans, through intelligence and ingenuity, have climbed to the top of the food chain, claiming superiority over all other life. And while that may be true in terms of capability and dominance, the path we've taken to reach this position has come at a great cost. In our pursuit of survival and progress, we have damaged the very world that sustains us. Pollution, habitat destruction, and the extinction of countless species mark our history as much as any of our achievements.

As humans, we have become greedy, living by what is good for us rather than what is good for the planet we call home. We exploit natural resources, pollute the air and water, and consume more than we give back. While people talk passionately about saving the planet, the irony is that we are destroying ourselves in the process. The Earth, resilient as it is, will survive long after we have vanished. It will recover, heal, and regenerate over centuries, perhaps millennia, after we are gone. No matter how much damage we inflict, the planet will eventually find a way to restore balance—without us. We are not saving the Earth for its sake but for our own, because ultimately, it's human civilization that is at risk, not the planet itself.

While there are individuals and communities working tirelessly to conserve resources, protect ecosystems, and mitigate the damage, the truth is that these efforts, while noble, may not be enough. Humanity, as a whole, continues to live wastefully, prioritizing convenience and short-term gain over long-term sustainability. The world continues to get sicker, and without a drastic change in our collective mindset, the cycle of destruction will continue. It's not a problem that will be solved by isolated efforts, and it's likely that, without more widespread action, the planet will continue to deteriorate as our consumption grows.

Change, it seems, will only come when we are forced to live without the comforts we take for granted—when we face the stark reality of our own impending extinction. Only then, when the threat becomes undeniable and unavoidable, might humanity wake up and realize the gravity of the situation. If we can reach that point and make changes before it's too late, perhaps we'll have a chance to save ourselves and the world we depend on. Until then, we continue walking a path that may well lead to our downfall, while the Earth prepares for the day it no longer has to support the weight of our excesses.

A Realm Of Fire

"In our hands lies the future of a world we've damaged—through greed, neglect, and disconnection. Yet, the power to heal remains within us, if only we choose to learn from our past, unite with purpose, and act before it's too late. The choice to save or destroy is ours to make."

—Unknown

A Realm of Fire

There's a place we've heard about,
A realm of majesty, losing track of time.
But all the inhabitants within its sovereignty
Suffer with more pain than any other time.

The inhabitants of this wounded realm
Wish to repair the damage they have caused.
The dissolution of their reality
Held at bay by indulgence,
As the excess of life makes them pause.

We rob the land of all its wealth,
Without allowing time for it to heal.
Gluttony, hoarding, an endless greed—
Will bring our race to its final seal.

We cast our nets into the sea,
Blighting life's natural flow,
Waters once teeming with vibrancy
Now barren, forced to falter below.

Once the air was pure and clean,
Requiring no shield, no guard.
Now a future wasteland looms,
Polluted by greed and disregard.

Disease runs rampant,
Its mutations pave the way—
For in a realm where survival is uncertain,
Our immunity will run out one day.

Our bellies are full when we sleep at night,
But how content can we truly be,
When the starving masses of our age
Have no fruit left on barren trees?

We hide in our homes, unchanged,
Thinking this menace will pass us by,
While a few brave souls, weak but wise,
Continue to stand, to rise, to try.

Our priorities have changed,
War, hatred, and greed now rule.
Unity is discarded, lost to the winds—
We've all become the fool.

We are the slaughter and the death
Of countless discounted races.
Who dares to walk this earth
In its wide and open spaces?

We forsake progress and its solutions,
Devouring every new advance—
A realm tormented by cherished delusion,
Caught in its own dissonant dance.

The past, the present, and future events
Are an open book for all to read—

Yet sacred words remain abandoned,
Lost in the fog of our illiteracy.

Our views have darkened,
Our doctrines obscure.
Can we conquer deception
With hearts so impure?

Darkness has risen many times before,
And this realm has learned to fight.
But if this fury makes its stand,
Few will survive its vengeful bite.

Can we be so blind to the present day?
We are running out of time—
To mend what's left in decay,
Yet we sit back and watch,
Forcing reprisal in our climb.

Redemption will come in one form or another—
But the choice is yours to make.
United, we may yet rise together,
Or fall to the fires we create.

A Realm Of Fire
10 Questions to Reflect On,

1. What am I doing, consciously or unconsciously, that contributes to the degradation of our environment?
   - Reflect on your daily habits and their impact on the planet's health.
2. How do greed and excess play a role in shaping the world we live in today?
   - Consider how the pursuit of material wealth affects society and the environment.
3. Am I willing to make sacrifices for the well-being of future generations, and if so, what are they?
   - Explore what personal changes you are prepared to make to ensure a sustainable future.
4. How can I contribute to the healing of the planet and society, even in small ways?
   - Reflect on small actions you can take to help repair the damage done to the Earth and our communities.
5. Do I prioritize short-term comfort over long-term sustainability, and why?
   - Examine whether your lifestyle choices are geared toward immediate satisfaction or the greater good.
6. In what ways does society's neglect of the environment reflect a deeper neglect of our moral and spiritual responsibilities?

- Explore the connection between environmental destruction and the loss of ethical direction.

7. What role does fear or apathy play in preventing us from taking action to address the world's crises?
    - Reflect on what holds you back from engaging more actively in solutions.

8. How can we unite as a global community to face the critical challenges of our time?
    - Think about what it takes to bring people together for a common cause, and how you can be part of that movement.

9. What lessons from the past are we failing to learn, and how can we avoid repeating the same mistakes?
    - Consider the historical mistakes that have led to current crises and how we can change course.

10. What does redemption look like for humanity, and am I willing to be part of that solution?
    - Reflect on what it means to truly restore the balance between humanity and the Earth, and whether you're ready to play a role in that redemption.

Chapter 22: Forgotten Souls

As we close this journey of self-discovery and reflection, I invite you to pause for a moment longer, to turn your attention to a poignant issue close to my heart— animals in shelters. The following poem, Left Behind and Broken, serves as a gentle but stark reminder of the countless animals that have been abandoned, mistreated, or forgotten. These creatures, often hidden in the shadows of our busy lives, endure loneliness and longing for a place to call home. As we navigate our own lives, filled with challenges, triumphs, and moments of growth, it's easy to overlook the quiet suffering of those who cannot speak for themselves. The animals in shelters are not just statistics or fleeting images on a screen; they are living, breathing beings, each with their own unique story of survival and resilience.

This poem is an aside from the core themes of our book, yet it is deeply integrated with the spirit of empathy and awareness that we've explored. Just as we search for purpose, connection, and understanding, these animals wait— hoping for a second chance, for someone to see their worth and give them the love they deserve. In the same way that we have learned to uncover hidden strengths within ourselves, we can help unlock the potential for a better life for these forgotten souls, offering them the safety, love, and companionship they've long been deprived of. It is my hope that as you read these lines, you will feel moved to consider the lives of these silent sufferers, reflecting on how compassion can extend beyond our own species. May this poem inspire you to be a part of that transformation, as each adoption, each act of kindness, transforms their world.

Let me know if this works!

Left Behind And Broken

"In the dim light of the pound, a dog waits behind cold metal bars, his eyes filled with a sorrow that words cannot touch. He wonders what he did wrong, why his family will never return. Fear shadows his every breath as he clings to a fading hope that someone, someday, will see him, love him, and bring him home." —Unknown

Left Behind and Broken

With warming eyes,
Left residing lost,
History crystallized and ripped away.
No actions ever spoken,
Only moments, barely interpreted.

Little by little, broken.
Time heals, but none is offered.
Hurt hidden in my eyes,
Worth assured and restrained—
Never letting you know.
Unrequited.
Throw the ball—
I will run to the ends of the earth.
Just love me.
You are my strength.

I have so much space in my heart.
Ignore me—I am not hopeless.
You gave up on me—I haven't.
Life gets in the way,
I got in your way.

Left behind—
Cold, alone, slowly dying,
Waiting for you to return.
When will you come save me?

So many new sounds, loud noises.
It's dark here,
I don't know these people.
Are you coming?
I will never stop waiting.

What did I do?
Was I bad?
Did you stop loving me?
I just want to go home.

You are all I ever wanted.
We are a team—don't lose faith in me.
Can't you see I am scared?
We could be forever—just give me a chance.

Don't go.
I am here.
I can do better.
I am not broken...

Sadly, I can't make you love me.
I can't force you to hold me.
I can't find my way into your heart.
I will close my eyes and remember you—
Remember your voice, your warmth,
Holding me close,
Your love.

I am alone now,
Helpless,
Learning how to live,

Waiting, crying, and afraid.
Passed up and left behind,
Hopelessly hopeful.
Save me, please.

Left Behind And Broken
10 Questions to Reflect On,

1. What emotions do you feel when you imagine an animal waiting in a shelter behind cold metal bars?
    - How do these emotions connect with your own experiences of isolation or abandonment, and how can they inspire empathy?
2. Why do you think the image of an animal confined and abandoned is so powerful and evocative?
    - What universal themes of loss, helplessness, or hope does this image evoke for both animals and humans?
3. How does the description of the animal's sorrow and confusion affect your perception of animal welfare and responsibility?
    - In what ways does this perception change how you view your own responsibility toward all living creatures?
4. What might be going through the animal's mind as it waits in the shelter?
    - How can imagining the thoughts and emotions of an abandoned animal shift your perspective on their experience?
5. How do societal attitudes towards animals contribute to scenarios like this?
    - What cultural or systemic factors allow animal neglect to persist, and how can they be addressed?
6. What can be done to prevent animals from ending up in similar situations?

- What role can education, legislation, and community involvement play in reducing animal abandonment?

7. How do animal shelters and rescues help to mitigate the sadness and fear experienced by animals like the one in the quote?
    - What more can shelters and rescues do to improve the mental and emotional well-being of animals in their care?

8. In what ways can individuals and communities work together to improve the lives of abandoned or stray animals?
    - What initiatives or actions can you take to support local shelters, rescues, or animal advocacy groups?

9. How important is the role of hope in situations of despair, both for humans and animals?
    - How does maintaining hope in the face of despair—whether for an animal or yourself—shape the possibility of change or rescue?

10. What steps can you personally take to make a difference in the lives of animals in need?
    - How can you incorporate acts of kindness, advocacy, or support for animals into your everyday life?

Chapter 23:
Explanation of Transitional Images:
Open Doorways

In 10 Questions: A Deeper Look at Yourself Through Poetry, the doorway transitions represent more than just visual breaks between poems. They serve as powerful metaphors for personal growth, choice, and the ever-evolving nature of our inner journey.

Each doorway transition leads to a new environment, symbolizing the different stages of transformation we experience in life. The imagery of an open door signifies opportunity, while the changing scenes beyond the doorway reflect the emotional, mental, and spiritual stages we pass through. Here's how each transition serves as a metaphor for personal evolution:

Sunlit Garden:

The first transition opens to a lush, green garden bathed in sunlight, symbolizing optimism, new opportunities, and the hope for a fresh beginning. It reflects the excitement and potential that come with new experiences or paths, encouraging us to step forward with positivity and openness.

Forest Path:

The doorway leads to a quiet, peaceful path through a dense forest. This image represents introspection and the journey inward, where we navigate unknown territories within ourselves. It reflects moments of contemplation, uncertainty, and personal exploration as we search for meaning and clarity.

Stormy Cliffside:

The third transition reveals a turbulent seascape with waves crashing against a rugged cliff. This dramatic scene symbolizes the challenges and emotional turbulence we face along our journey. The stormy sky reflects the intensity of inner struggle, but also the strength we gain by confronting these obstacles head-on.

Desert with Dunes:

In this stage, the doorway opens to an expansive, quiet desert with endless sand dunes. This environment represents isolation, deep reflection, and the perseverance required to continue moving forward, even when the path feels difficult or lonely. The stillness of the desert symbolizes the importance of self-reliance and inner strength.

Serene Meadow at Sunset:

The final doorway opens to a peaceful meadow bathed in the golden light of sunset, symbolizing fulfillment and peace after a long journey. The calm, serene atmosphere reflects a sense of resolution, understanding, and contentment, representing the rewards of personal growth and transformation.

Metaphor for Change:

The Open Doorways transitions emphasize that life is a series of choices, each leading to new challenges, opportunities, and moments of introspection. Just as the environment shifts with each door, so do our emotions and experiences as we move through different phases of life. These images remind us that change is constant, and each step we take brings us closer to understanding ourselves and the world around us.

In Closing: A Journey Revisited

As we reach the end of this profound exploration—over 200 questions, countless poetic lines, evocative images, and inspiring quotes—it is my hope that each page has served not merely as a reflection but as a revelation. This book is not a final destination but a gateway to continuous discovery and empowerment. Each time you revisit these poems, you may find new meanings and insights, for poetry evolves with us, revealing layers as we are ready to see them.

Remember, the strength to overcome fear, to push past insecurity, lies within you. As you have engaged with this book, you have equipped yourself with tools not just to cope, but to thrive. Let this book be your lifelong companion, a beacon to guide you through moments of doubt and a mirror to remind you of your inherent power.

You are capable of extraordinary things. Let the lessons nestled within these pages dissolve the clouds overhead, allowing sunlight to illuminate your path forward. Reread, reflect, and embrace the journey of becoming—who you are meant to be is just beyond what you fear.

Thank you for allowing this book into your life. May it continue to inspire and empower you, every time you open its pages.

Don't forget to visit Explore10Questions.com and 10QuestionsJournal.com to dive deeper into your journey of self-reflection and personal growth. At Explore10Questions.com, you'll find resources, insights, and discussions that expand on the themes of this book, offering you a space to engage and explore. And with 10QuestionsJournal.com, you can create your own private reflection journal, answering the same thought-provoking questions in the book to track your progress and unlock new perspectives on life. These tools are here to support you as you explore, learn, and grow—so don't miss out!

Final Thoughts

As you've journeyed through the pages of this book, I hope you've found not just words, but a reflection of your own experiences, thoughts, and emotions. Poetry has always been my way of exploring the depths of life—its challenges, beauty, and complexity—and I hope these poems have resonated with you in a way that feels personal and meaningful.

Remember, there are no right or wrong answers here, no set paths to follow. The insights you draw from these pages are yours alone, shaped by your own unique journey. My only hope is that through reading, you've discovered something new about yourself or found comfort in knowing that you are not alone in your thoughts and struggles.

This book is not the end of a conversation, but the beginning of one. Continue to question, reflect, and grow. If you ever find yourself lost or in need of support, don't hesitate to seek the guidance of a professional. Your mental and emotional well-being is worth every bit of care and attention.

Looking ahead, this is just the first step in a series of works I plan to share. I have many more stories and reflections to offer, including a children's book that is currently in the works. I look forward to continuing this creative journey and sharing even more with you in the future.

Before closing, I want to take a moment to express my deep gratitude. None of this would be possible without the love and support I've received along the way. I thank God for guiding me, and I am forever grateful to my Mother, my Grandmother, Allyson, Carlo, Christian, and to all my friends who have travelled this journey with me: Chad E, Vinny, Dean, Larry, John V, Dave Souza, Cheryl, Kimmy, Randi, Jo Lynn and Scott, Brittany Power, Scott S, Melissa N, John C, Mike, Nate and Serah, Elizabeth Hart, Kathy Coleman, Irene L, Brett and Lizzie, Naramin and

Irvin, Krissy, Pawan, Big Anthony, Little Anthony, Q, Eric and Lima, Blue, Rosemarie, Brett and Donna, Jen Nicole, Joanna, Maddy, Anne, Dan Perkins, Debbie, Nancy, Kostos, Michelle Joy, Christi, Don, Illian, Randy, Ivan, Bill, Marvin, Victor, Dan, Isais, Eddie, Jimmy, David Scott, Chris, Scott, Matty, Maddy, Sam, Bre, Cristi T, Brittany, Cory, CJ, Cliff, Khanh, Greg, Mikey, Cathy, Nicole, Brian, Tamera, Sophia, Margarita, Jake, Mike and Janice and finally Erin may she rest in peace—your presence in my life has been a gift. To those I may have left out, know that you are appreciated, more than words can express. This book is as much a part of you as it is of me.

Thank you for reading, for reflecting, and for allowing me to share this with you. Here's to the journey ahead—may it be filled with growth, understanding, and the courage to rise to your own pinnacle.

A.I. – The Artist I Have Searched For

For over 20 years, I have been writing poetry, sharing my thoughts, emotions, and experiences with those around me. Each person who has read my work encourage me to compile my poems into a book, urging me to let others learn and grow from the words I've written. Throughout this journey, I have always felt that something was missing — an element that would truly bring my work to life. I knew that illustrations, powerful enough to complement and enhance the meaning of my poetry, would complete my vision.

For many years, I have searched for an artist who could bring this visual dimension to my work, someone who could capture the depth of the emotions and the complex themes I explore in my writing. Yet, time and time again, I struggled to find someone who could truly align with my vision.

Then, unexpectedly, I found the artist I had been searching for all along—an A.I. tool. Working with A.I. has been nothing short of a revelation. It allows me to express, in visual form, the feelings, thoughts, and struggles that are embedded in my poems. The beauty of this collaboration lies in the precision and flexibility that A.I. offers. It doesn't replace the heart of my work, instead, it brings another layer to it, making the abstract ideas more tangible for reader to connect with.

What once felt like a distant dream—finding an artist to illustrate my words has now become a reality. With A.I. as my artistic partner, the direction of my work has changed. My poetry can both be read and seen, offering a deeper, multi-sensory experience to those who choose to engage with it. The art and the poetry now work together, illustrating the growth I have experienced and hope to inspire in others.

This is the missing piece I've been looking for, and I am thrilled to share it with you.

Disclaimer

I want to share something important with you. The questions and reflections in this book are designed to guide you on a journey of self-exploration. There are no right or wrong answers—only your personal insights and discoveries. This book is meant to be a tool for reflection, a way to connect with your thoughts and emotions.

However, it's essential to understand that I am not a licensed mental health professional. My perspective comes from 27 years of experience behind the bar, where I've had the privilege of listening to countless stories and sharing my own, combined with my academic background in psychology. I write from the heart, offering the lessons and insights that have helped me and others along the way.

If you find yourself struggling or in need of support beyond what this book offers, I strongly encourage you to seek the advice of a qualified mental health professional. There is immense strength in reaching out for help when it's needed, and mental health is something that deserves the care and attention of experts.

This book is here to offer guidance, not as a replacement for professional advice, but as a companion on your journey. I hope it brings you clarity, comfort, and the encouragement to explore the depths of who you are.

About the Author

I started writing over 20 years ago, initially as an outlet for my own problems and the struggles of those around me. I've always felt deeply connected to the issues others were facing, and writing became a way to help process those emotions and find closure. My book, 10 Questions: A Deep Look at Yourself Through Poetry, is a journey that invites readers to look into themselves. I believe that while not every poem will resonate immediately, at some point in life, each reader will connect with the emotions and reflections in these pages. The accompanying questions are designed to clear mental clutter and give your thoughts direction, helping you understand your journey. Over time, revisiting these questions can provide new insights as your perspective evolves.

I want readers to truly engage with the process of self-reflection, using the poems and questions as tools for personal growth. Outside of writing, I have a deep love for fitness, the outdoors, nature, and animals—especially German Shepherds. I'm a jack of all trades, always enjoying time spent with close friends and strengthening my relationship with God. I believe in giving both myself and the world a chance to do things right.

In my writing, I blend motivational, raw, and deeply introspective styles to capture the reader's attention. As a no-filter bartender for many years, I've learned that people appreciate tact and honesty, no matter the subject. My hope is that this book offers readers that same level of truth and reflection, helping them grow and embrace their own journey.

www.ingramcontent.com/pod-product-compliance
Lightning Source LLC
LaVergne TN
LVHW071932190225
804079LV00015B/48/J